Book of Plough

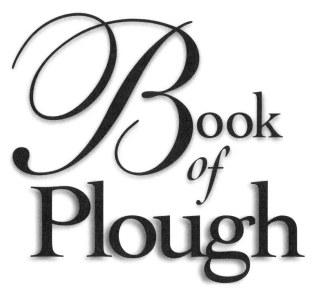

Book of Plough

Essays on the Virtue of Farm, Family & the Rural Life

JUSTIN ISHERWOOD

1996
Lost River Press, Inc.
Boulder Junction, Wisconsin

First Edition
First Printing, 1996

Jacket Art & Design: Julia Ryan @ Dunn & Associates, Hayward, Wisconsin
Interior Design: Galde Press, Inc., Lakeville, Minnesota
Editor: Mary KatharineParks, Grand Haven, Michigan
Printed in U.S.A. @ Worzalla Publishing, Stevens Point, Wisconsin

Library of Congress
Cataloging-in-Publication Data

Isherwood, Justin, 1946–
    Book of plough : essays on the virtue of farm, family, and the
rural life / Justin Isherwood.
        p.   cm .
    ISBN 1–883755–07–7 (hc)
    1. Farm life.   2. Family farms.   3. Country life.   I. Title.
S521.I88   1995
814'.54—dc20   95–40864
                                                                    CIP

For more information
contact the publisher at:
Lost River Press, Inc.
PO Box 620
Boulder Junction, Wisconsin 54512

**For a free color catalog
of other Lost River Press
outdoor and nature titles,
call toll free 1–800–366–3091.**

Contents

Plough

The farmer's symbol is the plow. Take a moment and say it any of the old ways; Old English *ploh,* Old Norse *plogr,* Swedish *plog,* Danish *ploug,* Polish *plug,* Old Frisian *ploch* or Russian *ploog.* The word has a curious, dull sound, as if the word stands for the sigh that is earth opened and rolled over, a sound we should expect of a tool capable of the furrow.

Strangely enough the plough originated at the same time in the Orient as it did in the Fertile Crescent ten to twelve thousand years ago. For the next eight thousand years the plough was the single most important instrument in the development of human civilization. The plough transformed a vaguely competent life form of wandering hunters and gatherers into an ever more survivable sort. The plough alone created the margin necessary for a succession of advances; language, number theory, and specialized labor that gave rise to village and city. The plough is the instrument of human birth.

I have wondered, as a farmer might, why the plough is not an altar piece. Why it is we hang relic flintlocks and muzzle loaders on the fireplace mantles and nary a one of us thinks to hang the ploughshare. Yet this the very fulcrum of our humanity for twelve millenia.

I have wondered too if it was a hunter weary of the chase who thrust his stone spear into the ground out of frustration with forever following the wild herd. Never home at night and missing the kids, this hunter who found the ground opened and his weapon become the spring tool. Like the plough, the seed in the beginning was accidental. It was the hunter who noticed that seeds followed broken ground differently than ground that wasn't broken. Then after a million years of following wild berries and wandering game it was over, and our hunter knew the home place at last.

The memory of the plough is well served by the Biblical account. The Garden of Eden symbolically represents the ancestral hunt. The elements are the innocence of the wandering hunter, his unknown nakedness is the vulnerability of the hunter. Sin was to stay in one place and eat the fruit of the furrow, to know the hearth of woman when the hunter ought be afield with the other hunters. The Garden of Eden is perhaps the story of the transformation from hunters to farmers. Banishment from the Garden was the loss of man's wildness, our innocence of the hunt and the closeness to fates and gods. The farmer was in control and less the supplicant for that. Did we think it was sinful because man was redesigning himself, his world, taking on the prerogatives of god? Was this then original sin? The hunt had always been the way, so the farmer felt very nearly sinful, less pure than before.

The bias for the old purity of the hunt persists in the biblical account of Cain and Abel. Cain was the farmer and Abel the herder and hunter.

"It came to pass, that Cain brought of the fruit of the ground an offering unto the Lord. And Abel, he also brought of the firstlings of his flock...And the Lord had respect unto Abel and to his offering. But unto Cain and to his offering he had not respect."

Yahweh apparently was not into vegetables. Cain marked the end of the ancient way of the hunt. Again the Bible goes on to say Cain sired Enoch and it was he who built the first city. Urbanity

then, and the farmer, were the mark of Cain. And all those prosperous farming villages of Babylon that followed, south of Ararat
in the broad Mesopotamian River plain, between the Euphrates
and the Tigris.

Plough Monday was celebrated by Saxon farmers, a day to
honor the plough. On this day ploughmen turned their coats inside
out and went door to door collecting pennies and loaves and roast
beef, apple pie and a kiss, were it offered. Any who did not con-
tribute had their lane ploughed over so their way was muddy until
the ground hardened again.

At night the ploughmen sang around kindling fires in their
fields. They raised toasts to their ploughs, "might they endure." A
toast to the warm spring earth, "may it also endure" and raised the
cup to the ox, to themselves, their mistresses, and wished them all
to endure. They laughed and lied and oiled their plough handles,
polished their coulters and slept among their fields. The Tuesday
after Plough Monday was holiday as well, a day to sleep off the
night before and wander the fields and pace out the center for the
back furrow. On Wednesday morning early, the venerable Reverend
met them with the Cross of Rome and stood across the field where
the Ploughmen had marked it. They then began the furrow, heading
straight as ox and man can, straight for the Lord's standard.

At the end of the first turning the ploughman looked over his
shoulder to see his furrow. The field's fate was cast. If straight it
was well. If crooked then too it was done and no ploughman
thinks to right a furrow once put. So it has been since Cain.

I ask you, should not the modern field also find Plough Monday and sing away the night, take supper there and raise the toast?
To the plough, to the beast that pulls and to your dooryard's mis-
tress. And on the morrow raise a standard at the far side, be it
cross, sword or panpipe as might lead your furrow straight. At the
end look over your shoulder and see how well the furrow has come.

The Planting

It is quite impossible to overstate the dawn. In the before dawn dark the ice-heaped hills lean against the horizon like the teeth of a rip saw, threatening the last fibers of the night. An hour yet till sun-up, but the farmer is tilted out of his retreat by the same pry that cants his North Country away from its winter. A planting morning. A day special from the rest, honored among the multitude of mornings and so the need to prepare like the bride or the priest.

The sun slips its rose quartz shoulder above the hills. It is the obligation of tillers and planters to watch the sun enter and ascend its unchallenged chair. On this morning the sun is both sovereign and compatriot whose meated chest slides into a sky of blue bib overalls. Come to work, and on this planting morning enter into the tasks of townships.

Planting has been with us too long, seen by too many eyes in arm's reach of a pencil, to be seriously orphaned. Planting is the recyclable beginning. Old failures are forgotten: the summers too dry or when prices were dim, unwashed mirrors of reality. It doesn't matter now, this planting is the original, the first of all days.

Planting is a different terrestrial with reclusive physics having little to do with supply and demand. Send spies to watch farmers.

Watch them touch the land's fertile belly and feel it jump in response, frightened and eager as he to enter a conspiracy of whispers and plows.

Planting possesses a meaning beyond the shape of kernel and hand. A wizened power is in the seed. A force we for all our literature and science treat the same, "worship" the same as less literate societies. "It" is raining; "it" is going to storm; "it" is dark. "It" has no antecedent. It is it. Definitions beyond such crude proximal attempts become difficult. Of what farmers know, "it" is the seed. In the township, the seed is the altar chalice.

A curiosity comes natural. How does "it" know the sun is warm and the sod turned on a soft welcome side? With what eyes does "it" see? With what toes does "it" touch earth? On inspection, the seed is a grain of sand, more pebble than life. Yet it does know, does feel the embrace and the doors of the tomb open and the pale limb of the cotyledon reaches out. Of resurrection ask no more than the seed. The seed knows no dying; from its cloth comes the only garment of paradise.

A potato is prisonered in a forgotten cellar corner, rolled away from the frying-pan fate of its companions. Spring finds it a burning bush. Fuses tricked from eyes in a place so dank and dim as to forbid fire. We think the old vegetable too wrinkled to produce the infant cry of spring. Yet it does. Its roving eyes have found caress. Testifying to an innate sexuality, the brazen back-seat hands of a drive-in movie spread in a democratic layer across the whole wild acreage of the living. Don't loudly ask the names of the appendages and pores. Neither avert your gaze from the supplicant genitalia of aspen, the succulent invitation of willow and the swollen passion of a maple branch. Instead fear the shame that makes you blind.

Try and source it. Take scalpel and incise the tissue to find the spark, the recalcitrant ember that each spring is whipped into fire. Always the need to go deeper, farther into the tissues to find the source. We are kidnapped by the search, haunted by the question; what is life? Odd, the seed that has life needs the company of stones, thin sands, loams and clays that do not. The seep we follow doesn't end at a mountain spring in a percolating swamp tucked among hills; life, like the water, begins still farther upstream.

What words are whispered in the seed's rendezvous with the ground? We wish to listen and hear what they have to say, one to the other. Eavesdrop on the chants, murmurs and incantations. That femoral gossip is what turns our requisite attention to Moon and Mars. The reason we send hired hands to dark outer rooms to hammer at rocks, to sift sands, to peer behind and beneath. It cannot be us alone. We don't want to be alone; the room is too big to go unshared. So we search for it, for the simplest sparks of it, hoping the glow will echo across the wide shadowed valley. We may guess what we will find, what shape the aliens will be, and the learned syntax of their tongue. A realization will humiliate us when by a distant mediocre star we greet a pine cone as brother, an elk as a lost twin and yeast mold as sure second cousin.

Geese define the grace of spring. Our children's children will marvel, when having visited a dozen silent orbs, to hear stories of geese that rode wings of wind and feathers, and prize an antique whittled goose call. They'll ask of the shape. "Did they really fly in wedges like adoring hands offered in prayer?"

The township holds full measure of what divinity is in the cosmos. Nothing greater will be found out there, perhaps nothing less. Odd how we look to neutron bombs and the supersonic murderous darts of humanity at its incompetent worst to teach us of power. Take the children away from the air shows, the parades, the martial music, the ribboned tanks that promise only blasphemy. Instead go to the field, a plain, undecorated country place with no bronze memorial, no plaque to commemorate the battle waged in the township. Watch the seed unfurl its flag. Watch it grow vertebrate and rear its sinuous life upright. Dare your own life be fueled with the same magnanimous trust, the same thrill of sunshine. Dare dance so delicate a ballet as the waist bending turn of compass flowers. Or the insidious genius of madly scribbling quack grass, or the sworn sand poverty of monkish camomile.

It is difficult to maintain a romantic ideal of farming, to remember the meanings when morning fades and drive chains break, clutches slip, gears rupture, bearings burn. A farmer is defined as much by his skinned knuckles as the dust in his pocket. The priest is always conscious of his life and the sense of celebration and ritual, motions pleasurable in themselves, enraged with meaning. The farmer has to remind himself that Work is Ritual, the unmasked reason. Doubtless other lives and other professions wed ritual and work, psychosis would be far more rampant were it not so. In each case is the hair-prickling sense of the near approach to compelling energies.

Good that a farmer should scratch open a nerve and touch it to his profession. The farmer, so knowing, is less carnivorous of his neighbors, less savage to the shape of land. The point is to be present and participate. To use shoulders and arms and legs. Tractors have little to do with it. Nor does the size of the farm: five acres may do as well as fifty or five hundred. We, who use tractors and planters that set rows in bunches, should spend one day, one hour planting potatoes with an elm branch. Or plant corn with an antique contraption more resembling a cane than a tool. Big tractors suppress by their very bulk nerve twinge and earth spasm. The hand planter with its wood handle and pouting steel mouth is a sure electrolyte that leaves the farmer trembling at the embrace. Object, to arrive at supper having been there. To have watched solar systems and suns kneaded from dusty ingredients and the simple seed birthing into the light of a common-issue star.

Planting rivets us to the ground sure as it did a thousand years or five thousand years ago. Greening is our planet's greatest trick. It sends us to find the same ability out there. For farmers it is enough to survive to supper, and the house blessed by the smell and dust of the planting.

The Sum of the Parts

C hanging points is a rainy day job. The tractor is tucked just inside the shed. Overnight it was forty degrees, now at 2:30 p.m. it's thirty-nine. They predict snow.

The radio is tuned to the Rib Mountain station and the Thursday afternoon concert, Barber's "Adagio for Strings." A steady west wind terrorizes the shed doors. The steel roof spreads rumors of snow and I am waiting for spring.

The whole countryside is waiting. Certain forays have been made at it. Cousin Jim down the road tried the disk last week in the field behind his house. Seen him from the bridge. One lap and he put it back in the shed. He meant to advance the idea in private. He shoulda known better.

Perhaps the most satisfying characteristic of farming and farm life is its rich sense of season. Distill that thought and the sense is of parts. A farmer is aware of earth as parts, partner, participation, and that he has an equal in creation. Take the common mold-board plow. It has more parts than you'd suppose; plowshare, lead bolt, land side, turn home, frog, mold-board, and frame. The plow has eight bottoms, the shares are changed every fifty to seventy acres if a rock hasn't spent it beforehand. At $20 each times eighty: $1,600 for plowshares at stony loam.

Part are the seed potatoes in the west shed, worth $35,000 on delivery. Two bulk seed trucks at $20,000 each; the plow tractor $78,000; the plow at $14,000, besides a disk; quackdigger and planting tractor $59,000. Which don't include the fertilizer truck, the '61 Chevy with a bad case of rust. On six cylinders it has to pinion and crawl up Moore Hill. The new one is red and has a radio, $24,000. A PTO gearbox attached to the transmission case drives the hydraulic motor on the boom-auger on the gravity box, $6,000 for the parts. There's the tractor with self-leveling front-end-loader at $19,000. Three sheds with cement floors, $80,000.

The potato planter is pulled by a four wheel drive John Deere 4450, hundred and forty horsepower on quadruple rear wheels, has a radio too. Loaded, the planter weighs eleven thousand pounds, which has to be pulled through eight inches of new plowed at three miles per hour. The seed-cutter was hand-made in Idaho by a jack Mormon married to a Navajo lady. He builds a dozen every year and delivers them to customers with his pickup truck. It's worth buying one to see his wife, she is a turquoise and silver beauty. Nineteen thousand dollars includes a spare set of knives.

Great grandad bought the first forty at $1.50 an acre. Was an awful price at the time, considering the parcel was cut-over and lumber companies had paid $1.25 including the timber. Just bought another 160 acres at $2,100 each. Has two center pivots, two high capacity wells, two diesel engines, and is handsome sandy loam even if the moraine end has a few rocks.

I left the farm eighteen years ago. I went to grad school, tried Minneapolis, Wausau, teaching, truck driving, and medicine. I came back fourteen years ago. The younger brother graduated from the university law and practiced seven years. He came back too. Number One stayed the whole while. Was he that changed the farm from Holsteins to vegetables. Pa hated to see the cows go but it was time for another man's dream. Besides that horizon brought his other sons back to the farm. Long days, dirty clothes, and haphazard pay. The sum can't be arrived at arithmetically.

Farming is ancient. I distrust the word, primal is close, and tribal. I use tribal a lot. Through the shed door I hear a flight of geese northing under a low sky. Yesterday the pond melted all the way across and it lay like a great blue eye inspecting heaven. This morning the first heron took an old and practiced course for the swamp. Farming is a life of parts. If you are a farmer you don't try to keep track of the list. Your only faith is to be part of it. The rain has turned to snow.

An Archeological Dig

I went on an archeological dig the other day. Well, not exactly a dig and not precisely archeological. I didn't use the meter grid, neither the whiskbroom or the mortar trowel, instead scratched away at the dirt with the toe of my boot. The discipline wasn't exactly science, something more prickly than science, too transient, too common, too subtle in the unforgiving gastronomy of farm fields.

Farmers don't openly acknowledge themselves archaeologists but they are and know they are. It comes as a consequence of fields and those who tend them and witness in person the digestive act. It is less a crime of fields than indifference, of homestead and chimney scattered like the till from a remorseless glacier. Farm archeology is simple theater, no anguish, no memorials except the brow of where the fenceline was once, evidence that another tiller held the field differently. It is also the spilling of every odd-ball mechanical whose broken bits litter the earth many generations after; digger link and horseshoe, ox shoe, square nail, wrench, boot heel, fence staple, cant hook, axe head, jackknife, arrowhead, all in the same and haunted ground.

It has been forty years, give or take, since the last occupants of this field lived here. Their name as I recall was Howe, or some-

thing like Howell, or Howl. They dwelled here and in country
fashion the location came to be known as the Howe Place, a half
mile east of where the country school stood. I remember Jane, I
think her name was Jane, she attended the one room school with
the rest of us, there were ten altogether. Jane was thin and semi-
transparent as little girls sometimes are. She had long black hair
and dark bright eyes, her shoes always polished, almost too polished, and she had a tooth that crossed another in the front of her
smile. I think I should yet recognize her smile.

Jane was different from the rest of the kids at school. Jane was
a moth. All the other kids in school knew she was a moth, which is
too bad because she'd have made a pretty butterfly. Jane was a
moth because she lived in the little house down the road. I realize
this doesn't sound like much explanation but we all knew Jane was
a moth just the same.

The rest of us were farm kids and dwelt in fat, white farmhouses with oak-floored porches and samurai-like boxelders
guarding the house and enormous barns with cats in the haymow
and long tentacles of sheds and chicken coops layered in gun nitro
and pig styes that warped the atmosphere and corn cribs, woodsheds, brooder houses, fields and fencerows, woods and more
fields and the marsh for hay when there was drought. The Howe
place was sixty acres entire, jackpine scrub included. It was dab
farming, weeds mostly, a tiny, drafty house, maybe an emaciated
boxelder or two. I kinda recall a haphazard tree and pitcher pump.
Jane Howe was a moth because the place she lived was so blamed
mortal. The place had no chance, hardly a pulse, so shallow-
breathing, this translucent little house. In the winter the Howe
house looked plain awful, worse than any farmhouse ever, like it
was lost from a flock. The windows quivered in their frames and
there weren't no cellar either, no subterranean furnace to stoke
with whole trees, no root cellar, no shelves with fruit jars and

pickles and braided onions and cow's tongue in brine. The Howe place had no cunning, no instinct for survival, so Jane was a moth and we knew she was a moth and she couldn't last. I was in the second grade.

Farmers are archaeologists where no one else is or cares to be an archaeologist. Our tool is the plow and our practice of turning the pages backwards. Some ignore the text, dismiss the passages as just another chore. After all, it is better this way, tractors ought not to acquire memories. Not that it is cruel, it's life and how life earns the right and is called life and not the other.

The plow turns out the relic shard, a bit of pottery, and at a glance the ploughman sees it as it was before. The house stood on the gentle swell of sandy ground, the evidence scattered all around. A blackened brick, a lump of mortar, a nail. Wise farmers advise their sons and daughters not to get off the tractor. They know why this is wise, and there are acres yet to plow. Besides, it is past, done, do not look back at the pages in the book of the field. The tractor is buoyant and the reason the farmer can rise over memory.

The Howes moved the next year. The place was sold to a neighbor who burned the house, uprooted the boxelders, filled in the well. We all knew it was for the better. This is the way to improve the gene pool of butterflies, by ridding the fields of little houses that made you cold just to look at them.

Jane was a moth like those that collect on the windows during the cold nights of fall, their bright eyes tight against the glass. Attracted to the light they freeze to death on the window pane and are swept off the porch in the morning. If only they weren't so inquisitive, so drawn to the light of farmhouses, if only they had stayed where they knew how to survive.

That house could never have survived the field. It had no

chance, her father knew nothing of farming. It is hard to understand why they came; we were just kids yet knew the Howe place
didn't have a prayer. The next year Jane was gone and the place
she lived uprooted and burned. We knew it couldn't happen any
other way.

The artifacts seemed to fit the field now, no longer bitter. Bits
of window glass and a crushed door knob sorta match the gravel
and stones of the outwash. But another thing broken to bits by
something bigger and colder and washed in the stream of that reason. On the rise of ground where the house stood, the relics glint
in the sun like the other gravels glint, and a ploughman might pass
them without thinking. Perhaps the better for his ignorance.

For the better part of two generations, the Howe place has been
a field, a center pivot where the house stood. For all the former
fragility of the house, it is curious how resistant are its pieces.
Every year the plow turns up another foundation stone, just when I
think I have seen the last, another one is brought to the surface.
The remains of their midden litter the field. This is why archeology occurs at all, this is how moths survive despite their fragility.
Scattered among the furrows, broken yet intact enough to haunt
the farmer. Like I said, wise farmers never get off their tractors.
The field is not entirely supreme for the furrows keep spitting up
pot shards and moth bones, unlikely as that seems.

Archeology is impolite. I know things about the Howes I ought
not, knew them by what is forever gossiping behind them. How
they heated the house with coal, or tried to—must have cost a for-
tune to try—because traces of coal are scattered among the soft
curls of the new furrows.

I have found thick Red Wing crocks. Howes had lots of crocks
and by the remnants they were the large crocks, pickle crocks and
kraut crocks, a piece of dinner plate with two green rings at the
rim, plates thick enough for bulletproof. Coffee cups, milk bottles,
water glasses, the core of carbon battery, and the severed brown

lips of bottles, my suspicion is beer. Quart size, which brings another observation, quarts either because the man drank so rare, or quarts because he drank so often.

Ceramic light fixtures identical to the modern fixtures. A piece of blue-purple glass, maybe of Vicks VapoRub, the last medicine man. Before television and "more doctors recommend" aspirin cures, the remedy was VapoRub. I still use it myself on the theory if the body is made inhospitable enough, the pathogen will leave out of disgust. This the same reason defenders of feudal castles in a last desperate act burned everything they cared to defend.

If the field has won it has not forgotten the moths among the butterflies. No farmer can bear witness to how a field takes and scatters and fail to understand the field shall come in the same mood for him, his time, his place, bulldozed, burned and scattered, only the shards left to speak. So the farmer, despite his rare, great and heaving beast, though suited in his armor and safe in sight of his barns, knows he too is a moth. For the field tolerates no butterflies.

The Hired Man's House

A black asphalt crosses the Buena Vista marsh in formal precision to the grid lines of range and township. The melancholy dimension of the marsh permits roads an unimpeded design. Except for Coddington, a line of sand dunes that mars the otherwise perfect symmetry of the marsh. Coddington makes the road squirm. Roads on the moorland may well be straight but suffer other indignities. Frost mainly, and spring pockets, high water and a spongy soil.

Ted Jensen is a farmer. His land title begins just this side of the squiggle of the town road at Coddington. Ted bought the old muck farm experiment station from the state of Wisconsin when the powers that be figured there wasn't a future in muck farming. The buildings are well situated on the high ground of the sand dunes, whose existence testifies to the direction and ferocity of the glacial flow some ten thousand more-or-less years previous. Among oaks, the building site is as good as can be expected particularly for the marsh. The barn and the out-sheds are painted a butterfat yellow, reminiscent of a time when fluid milk was slop for the hogs and the Guernsey cow stood for progress and solvency.

Building sites are hard by on the Buena Vista Marsh. Winter holds a vendetta there, taking indecent liberties on cold nights.

Level ground conspires with dark prairie respirations. What is but a wisp of vapors in the hill country is brooding on low violence on the flats of the Buena Vista Marsh.

A morning in the village at ten below will be sixteen below on the marsh. Thirty-six is magnificent on the moors at forty-eight below. Inhabitants of the marsh, if any can be said to be, are aware of a cruel distinction between themselves and the villagers. Believing as they must that life on the marsh at the mercy of wind, muck, and thermometer puts hair on the chest. The ladies of the region thought the more cuddlesome for it.

Ted Jensen has been called a liar too often at the barbershop. Since 1934 he maintained the U.S. Commerce Department's weather station, whose calibrated recording thermometers were solid verification of his honesty. Temperatures that are strictly according to Hoyle and government thermometers, in a louvered white box set on stilts fifty paces below the house where the muck touched the hem of the sand dune. In 1951 the government sent an additional set of thermographs, which lent an interesting new strategy to the whole plot line. Centigrade Ted Jensen found could be utilized in wicked wonderful moments. In numeric terms, winters are the colder for it. Thirty-two Fahrenheit becomes 0 Centigrade. Minus 13 became a nifty minus 25. When the subject raised is spiny hide at the feedmill, it paid gloriously to have computed the calculations beforehand. The response had to appear nonchalant. "Last night? Ah, let's see....was 30 below exact." Left them breathless and silly with their meager 22 below. With practice Ted Jensen could say it without scrubbing the floor with his eyes and ruining the effect. Took practice though.

Jensen's hired man went by the name of Nels Piedric. Nels wasn't his first name but that's what he preferred and that's what everyone called him. The name had a genuine sound to it.

Nels had an uncommon sense of self. What theologians call

personhood and politicians call charisma. A characteristic that in
the township is knowing whether your feet are on straight and your
zipper at full mast without looking. Or at least not caring one
whiskcr if it weren't entirely so. Nels was on in years. Openly partial to whittlin', chaw, and hot apple pie. Here was a man who
knew the sunny side of the barn from the shady.

Nels Piedric worked for Ted Jensen, taking his pay in board
and occasional cash money to acquire the spiritual condiment of a
tin of smoking tobacco. Nels would have seen retina-to-retina with
most mystic eclectics, if at slight variance in the provisions.

Nels was not what you'd overtly call a hard worker. He knew
better. He worked as hard as the task demanded and by some
instinctive process usually found methods to diminish the octane
requirement. His was a near divine love of horses. Mowing hay is
an example of a fine and boring job. The avowed purpose of
proper mowage is to keep the corner true and square. A process
facilitated in the age of tractors by jamming the brake hard and
levering the snout over. Tractors had a tendency to over-steer, a
condition not improved by the lack of power steering. Unlike tractors, horses didn't require steerage. A well and proper team after a
couple acquaintance laps could take the corners themselves, which
allowed the teamster near perfect freedom, whether of observation
or slumber. Nels loved horses.

Time came Nels should take things easy, or easier. The alterna-
tives were to look up his family, rumored to be somewhere in
Pennsylvanie or to a punishment nearly as bad, the old folk's home
in the city. Nels being a wee independent wanted neither of the
possibilities. Instead hinted he'd like to build a place of his own.
Knowing full well a man like Ted Jensen paid rabid attention to
hints and clouds.

The Buena Vista Marsh had its share of tax delinquent land.
By sixth sense farmers know where the delinquent parcels are,
should a year have a surplus of cash money. Ted bought a lot on

the dune ridge of Coddington for seventy-five cents and paid the
back taxes of two dollars and thirty-one cents.

The lot was in a subdivision called Pine Island. A speculator
had plotted the sand dune nearly fifty years before, anticipating a
land rush from people wanting pretty bad the singular smell of
muck. A smell catalogued between onions and rutabagas, neither
totally annoying nor completely pleasant.

The marsh is favored by aspen trees called for some unknown
and likely unknowable reason, popple. Popple as a species has
what might be called a taste for liquor. Not at all the upland
refinement of oaks, which seem to wet their whistle so inocca-
sional as to appear totally temperate. Water is never far away on
the Buena Vista Marsh. The region being six feet lower than the
highlands. Aspen prefer the taste of such territory and the solitary
life. The tree has a certain advantage with its pale bark. The
vaguely green hue like that of a child too well fed on carnival
candy. The over-easy green prospers the tree despite any routine or
tardiness of spring. As a tree aspen is vigilant. Laying quick claim
to any field a farmer might turn his back on. Finding on his return
the big-hearted leaves of popple scattered mischievously among
brome grass and timothy.

Ted Jensen bought the plot on Pine Island when his woodlot
was brim over of popple and sending emigrants across his pasture.
Natural then the house he built for Nels Piedric was of popple
logs. A decision not so much of Jensen's mind but the rumination
and conclusion that is the thinking of the land. Ted Jensen's land,
the muck and moors of the Buena Vista Marsh.

Ted Jensen was the approximate sort of person to see the situation, then answer it with a minimum of fuss. Most account it to his
Swedish bloodline and being so gosh damn stubborn as to let society have its way. His father was famous in local legend; seems he
purchased a wooded forty and cleared it with axe, shovel, and a
sodden shirt. The story and the fame goes, without benefit of

horse or ox. It was suggested he could well have afforded an ox but felt the place had to be earned, inch by dog-damned inch. Ted could too, when knowing the need, have built a shack of two-by-fours and shiplap. That would have violated a compact. Broken something between father and son: do for yourself and use your own body as a lever and create something out of nothing because it is cheap and because it put meat on yah. New muscle layered in the shoulders and a kind of meat gained in a farmer's head and the way he thinks and what is between a man and a place.

Ted cut the aspen logs early that spring. Fifteen each for the sidewalls, half for the ends and floor joists and rafters. The length simply paced off, no need to measure. Big limbs saved for stove-wood and the bark peeled. On a Saturday with his son while the aspen was still slimy from the barking they laid up the logs. Easy work chopping half-round notches so the logs set snug against one another. Two rooms, living and kitchen. On Sunday morning they set the roof boards, rolled out the tarpaper, hung the door and set three windows. Monday before supper they laid a brick chimney. A week after the walls were chinked with a mixture of mortar, limestone, and horse manure.

Furniture they procured, a davenport, a battered table, two dis-similar chairs, one chest of drawers, a mattress, pitcher pump, and a blue enameled four-hole kitchen stove. When Nels moved in, a box of groceries was on the table; tea, bacon, bread, salt and potatoes. Ted had squared a garden spot, rooted it out with his Farmall and planted sweet corn, a row of peas, beans, cucumbers, and summer squash. A pile of firewood ricked at the back door and an old double-bee, chomped off for a stovewood hatchet hung on the wall.

The place was given what protection as jack pine and scab oak afford. A luxury on the Buena Vista Marsh where winter is a grudge fight. Nels continued to work for Ted during the summers. Coming to work instinctively about time the hay was ready to bale. Or miraculously, when one of those unnamed bits buried in the multitude of a machine broke and the day went off and wounded from there and needed to be shared. Nels walked the short way through the woods on the dune ridge. Helped feed and water the cows, lug pails, and carry his share of the conversation. Showed up to unload those invisible burdens that selectively prey on farmers and otherwise get invested into cuss noises.

Depending on who tells the story, it is remembered Nels was married. Some don't think it was a marriage at all. Rather an arrangement of convenience; he called her his mail-order fancy, seems their mutual ambition was discovered in a love-lorn column. That of course was on the second attempt. The first wouldn't spend the night. Wanted to go home soon as she saw the profile of that moor prairie and that god-curious little house. The lonely countenance of the Buena Vista Marsh is not known to advance confidence. Neighbors said Nels spent an endowment on taxis that night. Town at some distance and art of negotiation being what it is. "Take another look, you'll like it" approach. She did and didn't. It was the marsh, most thought. Something more than lonely, closer toward sinister or ill-boding. Perhaps the idea of the bed under an eighteen-light school window set side-long. Maybe the wash water from the barrel cistern beneath the floor, a long-handled dipper lowered through a trap door the method of procurement. The idea you might have to excuse passage between a gathering of spiders taints water for some.

The second one stayed. She liked it. Liked the very and whole idea of it. Of bread baking in a blue enamel stove. The wind eddying among the jackpine and the smell of jacks after rain and gruff flavor of the scab oak of Pine Island at Coddington in the middle of the Buena Vista.

Mark Twain said gettin' old is one of the easiest things he ever did. Said he didn't know if he was good at it, lacking any previous education in how it should be done or how to be prosperous in its consequences. Mark Twain didn't say that. Attributing quotes to

Mister Clemens whether he said them or not lends any statement considerable charm. Its credibility is already reconnoitered. Neither is it a lie outright. Clemens surely would've said such if he thought on it. As any cigar biter knows, lies are something that tain't true, not something that might be.

Getting old is easy if not always gentle with its practitioners. The matter is complicated in a world that values the new and the antique though not much in between. New has to do with honeymoons and Christmas. Antique is a tool handle without a head, kept for a shape beyond usefulness. Old just ain't fashionable when applied to people. Nobody wants to get old. Old things are broken and ill-maintained and consigned to a variety of landfills.

Ted Jensen knew of the infectiousness of age. Knew too the old belong to the place that made and used them. Not shipped like cattle to an exile, prisoners of their own passage. Ted knew retirement and pensions had to have a direct answer. Nothing maybe or somewheres else but right here exactly at this spot whether it was the Buena Vista or not.

The hired man's house is empty now. Kids have come and by an ancient formula rocked out the windows. The roof leaks. The door is off the hinges and deer mice hold squatter's rights in the mattress. It is as it should be. The mold and red lichen taking back their answer, the simple solution. Popple grows like weeds in the char soil of the Buena Vista Marsh. After the first hard frost popple are set to yellow fire. The leaves flutter and wave as if trying to attract attention like school children who know the answer. A regard is indelible.

At the Stillness
of Families

War, all wars, get a lacquer finish. Maybe no one intends it but this is the way it is. I don't know why. Leave a war to sit on a windowsill awhile, a war that killed off a generation and scared the rest to death, and sooner or later someone will take out the old uniforms and shine up the buttons and parade around in the guise of that war like it never bit off anyone. I don't know why.

My Grandma Fletcher had a war chasing her. Every time the family sat down to a dinner, whether Thanksgiving, Christmas, Easter, the Fourth of July, a meal where prayer was considered prerequisite and everyone dunked their heads under the gaze of god and eternity, and just before the words, came the stillness of families.

A stillness my grandmother couldn't stand. It was the same every time, as long as I knew her, she'd cry. The tenderest, most bashful sob you ever want to hear. We all knew she didn't mean to, she never made us wait, just dried those tears on her apron and went on, the trail they made down her face glinted, in a moment they too were gone. The stillness was over.

I never knew Uncle Jerome who was the source of this. He was killed the winter before I was born, died on an island in the western Pacific, part of a volcanic chain of no real worth except that February when everyone knew its name. A photograph of Jerome and his younger brother Kingsley stood on the piano in my grandmother's house since early in the war. I remember how that photograph of a smiling Marine corporal cast a shadow in the room, how after he was killed the parlor in the farmhouse was rarely used. How that room always seemed a little colder than the rest of the house though it was right next to a cast-iron grate the size of a tractor wheel. It was as if the warmth of life was not for that room. Nothing was ever moved there and it retained smells, wax and window cleaner, rag rugs, smells of pumice and cordite.

The stillness before prayer was the only time grandmother cried and the only time I ever met and knew my Uncle Jerome. He came back in that increment between bowing our heads to prayer and Grandma Fletcher's tears.

Many times I saw him in this instant with the rest of the Marines in that landing craft. I sat behind him and looked over his shoulder, the steel deck slippery and the craft battered by the sea until it approached the shore and then the sea calmed. How the fear was lumpy and hard to swallow and then it too smoothed out like the sea. The air smelled of smoke and sea, and a smell like you remember picking rock and they broke against each other.

For years Uncle Jerome came. Wandered in at that moment and I again looked over his shoulder that February morning in the stillness between prayer and tears. I had not known fear's smell was like warm meat and gravy, and the knowledge your life is on the menu.

With the prayer over, Jerome faded away and did not return again except at the next stillness of the family. This now many years ago and so many members of the table gone, and with them the presence of Jerome on an overcast February day at Iwo Jima.

I have often wondered if we all saw the same thing, a fleeting glance over the side of the landing craft, the helmets and rifles, the smell. Did others see him die too as a shell hit and everything went dark except for a lingering hiss of the sea?

The silence in the family is filled with others now, none have the same clarity or the same reason for it as Uncle Jerome on a morning in February, 1945. How we all know how the western Pacific smells. How we all knew why Grandmother cried.

Cures for Drought

Serious drought is a difficult consensus, being as sand farmers are inclined to declare drought several weeks before the loam farmer is prepared to declare drought. Neither does this include yet the clay farmer who is barely into tractable cultivation before his sand and loam neighbors are hosannahing claims of serious dry. The problem caused by this lack of unanimity toward drought is the uselessness of prayer to correct drought.

Ask any cleric as to the truth of this remark. One person, him being a sand farmer, praying for rain isn't gonna get it. Neither will an entire congregation of sand farmers. This is the reason that in the nearly 150 years of the Plover Episcopal Method church, the one by the railroad tracks, its membership was shy of farmers. Because any farmers attending would have been sand farmers only, whose combined power of prayer couldn't incite rain in Borneo.

This is the reason Pa affiliated with the Liberty Corners kirk, there being a mix of sand and loam farmers whose united prayer power was more like the required length of necessary wrench. Why the churches of the world do not understand prayer can't and will not work unless it is cross-pollinated I did not understand as a kid and I do not understand now.

Stands to reason if you want prayer to gain the floor of God's

Parliament, you had to occupy more space in the lobby than those prayers offered by sand alone. Sand prayer puts God in the untenable position of raining on one set of forties while not touching the neighbor over the moraine. It's unrealistic. Which isn't saying God can't do it, but clouds aren't the easiest things to herd as the Bible amply relates. During the Flood, God intended only rain enough to drown the sinners. Any more is a waste of water. Good two-day rain is all that is necessary what with folks cohabiting and sinning pretty much like they still do, as riverbank villagers. A week of solid rain surely been enough. It rained forty days. Meaning two hundred feet of water over the last drowned sinner. Proves God can throw the switch but the rest of rain is up to the cloud, which ought lead to caution in the use of prayer. Farmers know this. It is why intelligent farmers will not pray for rain. They understand God better than the preacher who prays for anything without regard to the sort of climatic mayhem as will result.

This is why farmers don't ask God to cure anything because they know the world has loose steering linkage. More likely a paddle than a steering wheel. Which at 1,000 miles-an-hour through the cosmos, arriving at a particular destination isn't any too certain.

The failure of prayer for farmers doesn't prevent them from attempting cures for drought but using the same sleight of hand a bidder uses at an auction. In particular when they are paying too much for something but want it anyway and so kinda hoping the auctioneer notices and kinda hoping he don't. Farmers don't pray so much as wiggle their discomfort.

One of the classic cures for drought is to set a late model pickup truck in a field overnight with the windows open. This is supposed to be a temptation rain can't resist. So is mowing down more hay than the farmer can possibly bale in two consecutive days.

I know of farmers who have four days of hay laying on the ground. Efficient baling has nothing to do with it. They are asking God, or the sub-God in charge of nimbo-cumulus, to mind their instruments and teach the farmer with four days worth of hay down a good lesson in agriculture. Ain't prayer at all. It's something but not prayer.

I know of womenfolk who have been washing clothes for a week solid, hanging them on the line, leaving them out over night. This is supposed to be a terrible temptation for rain. They have gone so far as to rewash what they washed the day before. One farmer's wife has left the same clothes on the line since the first of May. This on the main road yet. Some believe this is too brazen, saying there's a point at which temptation is more insult than temptation. I haven't seen any drought cures of this caliber myself but it could be. That God might take insult at this ruins my estimate of what kind of fella God is. Seems to me being the biggest pair of pliers this side of the Big Bang requires a high tolerance for insult. Despite the lack of scale in the comparison, I know from having kids myself that God has a pretty high resolution filter on the matter of impurity and insult.

Superstitious people used to sacrifice virgins to encourage rain. It did not on the other hand foster virginity. There is a minority interpretation that when Abraham took Isaac to the mountain to kill him, he didn't do it for worship as much as rain.

It takes serious bait to cure serious drought. That much we know. In so much as it hasn't rained on four days of cut hay, neither on the wash hanging out since the first of May.

We know, too, we don't want all the preachers of Wisconsin, Minnesota, and Michigan Territory turned loose in prayer, being as that is probably what caused the flood in the first place—overzealous prayer directed at someone else's sin. What we need then is something that looks like prayer but ain't. Myself I thought every center pivot in the township going at once was the sufficient substitute; guess not.

Maybe if we all went back to AM band radios, whose reception a good lightning storm can obliterate? Or if we took our half dozen most favorite books to the woods and left them over night? Or maybe spend a night in the woods ourselves without benefit of tent. Another thing as attracts rain is a load of new dug potatoes sitting unprotected in an open bulk box. Leaving the breech cover open on the mailbox is a good target, too. Ten thousand miles of rural route with open mailboxes ought bring rain without actually getting on our knees. And I've got a front-end loader with a sensitive ignition; spill the dregs of two teacups in Bevent and the thing won't start. Good as a Sioux medicine man with an eagle bone whistle for inspiring rain. I haven't set that tractor out over night because it is foolhardy and brazen. At last resort all the sand farmers and those of loam could show up at St. Adlebert's, which is Junction City and clay, but that's prayer as would provoke a cure but kill the patient. Like the Bible says, "and the rain was upon the earth forty days and forty nights..." and I can't swim for heck.

Shop

S unday afternoon, I had shut off the wire welder and had leaned back to contemplate the universe. Or what of it was available to view out the farm shop, which faces the south forty to cousin Jimmy's twin Harvesters and the woods. Beyond, the creek and the muckmoor of the Boney Vieux. It struck me how elemental is the farm shop to agriculting. Actually it didn't strike me as much as floated past.

Most people when they think of agriculture idioms do not recognize the farm shop as a central act or plot of agriculture. The visual farm is made of tractors, broad fields, barns, center pivots, grading sheds, gandy boxes, fertilizer by the ton, chemicals by the barrel, hydraulic hoses by the furlong. The farm image is of barns, steel sheds, and ploughs not shops. It was my sabbath thought that the central entity of the farm in America is the shop and these shops have a good deal to do with staying in business, in particular the agriculting business.

The claim does not follow that any furrow-practitioner with a farm shop is thereafter guaranteed absolution from fiscal harm. The proximity between the shop and solvency is not quite that tight. The fiscal decapitation can happen to the farmer whether he has a shop or not. The disclaimer noted, the presence of a farm shop has a vital relationship to remaining in business while other farmers are shipped off in the great and unkind cattle trucks, after which they are cut up and rendered into urban man.

Every farm magazine, if it has an honest witness of its laity, has the four or five basic ingredients. First is the mandatory discussion of new approaches: seeds, methods, supplements, exposés on stray voltage. Most rural magazines also make an attempt at humor, mostly out-of-date jokes recycled from '40s-era *Reader's Digests;* beyond is the preacher's column. A Reverend Bob who is no more inspired and high octane in his column as from the pulpit (I have an admittedly low opinion of preachers). What else? The farmwife column with recipes, something on pattern making, advice about stress management, using computers, managing the farmbooks. Farm magazines have ads, about the dumbest sort you are ever likely to see anywhere. On heavy gauge paper and using the best color spread in the entire magazine, they portray a verdant field of soybeans. Out of the middle of this field arises an enormous can of name brand herbicide, like an enameled King Kong. The image is supposed to sell farmers on the chemical's ability to control foxtail grasses.

The real test of any farm magazine is the fix-it page, and the reason farmers subscribe in the first place. Editors use the gimmick: "Farmers, send us your time-saving ideas and we'll pay you $10." Ten dollars! When the village hack who wrote the rehash about stray voltage got $300! Fix-it is usually the last page in the magazine and the first thing that practitioners turn to. Forget all the mumble-jumble of computer technology, Bovine Growth Hormone and gene splicing; none of it matters as much as a few clues on how to fix some flapping mechanical.

Barns have been declared the bosom and teton of the farm country. We have offered other worship: big white farmhouses and in a mixed order, haymows, sheds, coops, and cellars. All lend to the hospitable nature of rural existence. Many of these are offered up on the account of their shelter and preservation of farmers. As if barns and ploughs and root cellars have souls, or at least some capacity to enliven a soul. Less a Christian sense of soul as a black-jive kind of soul as might inhabit and equalize life. Soul as defined by hot blackberry pie. If you don't hold that blackberry pie has soul and deserves a place in heaven along with the replicated, mass-produced souls of Christianity then you won't believe me when I add another, the farm shop.

My first memory of the shop was my father's, in the north stall of the granary. Pa had burned down his earlier shop and why he did not burn down this one is proof of his personal luck. This shop being the same altar where we changed oil, anointed zerts, and welded. The other half of the granary filled with white oats and feedmill dust as explosive as TNT. Why the place did not explode in a Nazi blitzkrieg was proof of something I won't jiggle any to guess at.

The welder is the real center of agriculture. To heck with the plough, the seed, the herbicide, or nitrogen fertilizer. How often it restored our soul, our days, our neighbors. Well it might be the most haphazard fix imaginable, nearer glue than molten weld. Never mind, the result was the machine went back to the field, the day kept its pace, and the bank account remained unscathed.

A farmer with a welder on his back has a better chance at solvency than the farm pilgrim who preaches software. Something is in that blaze of sparks and incandescent iron, in the smoke of ionized gases, a sensation of agriculture as repairable, survivable, open to modification. A dividing line between not only getting through the day but getting to the bottom of the ledger and still standing upright on the plus side. In the shop the farm is reborn, at least resuscitated, somewhere between the welder, the grinding wheel, and the ballpeen hammer. Maybe the fix isn't up to factory specs but it works. Covered with grease, it works real well. Name the implement, it has been to this altar of healing.

If the farmers come in different kinds, and I suspect they do, then these shop kind are my folk. They are less tractor drivers and herdsmen as Yankee inventors and greaseballs who on more than one occasion picked Lazarus right out of the ground, fixed him, and got another day's work out of what all else thought was plain dead junk. Give me any average batch of farm tinks, a supply of cutting torches, and one loaded wire-feed-welder and with these kind I'll go to hell; and if they don't lower the temperature, they will at least improve the ventilation. When it comes to tribe and tartan and that self-congratulating lump of kindred folks you want to belong to, this is the branch of farmshipers to whom I doff my hat and swear my faith. The fixers with the blackened knuckles and sinister fingernails, the guys with the hair singed off their forearms.

Lingering in the shop on Sunday morning is not quite so irreverent as you might suppose. This is Genesis as I know it. To sit and look out the shop door is Sabbath enough, to think on what is made, what is unmade, and what needs fixing.

Corn on the Cob

The subject is mundane and wayward besides. Still, if there is a vegetable as inspires dreams, it is corn on the cob. Not broccoli, Brussels sprouts, okra, peas, beans, cauliflower, neither artichokies, spuds, kohlrabi or spinach.

When it comes to food and food preparation, there are many things I do not understand, notably the French. I have friends who cook and like to try to persuade my farmer heart with sauces. They will marinate pork chops in sugar. It is a French recipe, they say. I knew that.

The French treat every food as if it has been dead too long. They paint every meat, every root, every morsel with a membrane of antithesis. No meat, no fruit or vegetable tastes of the original source. The sauce is supposed to add enlightenment. It doesn't.

Texans do the same thing to food. But at least you can trust Texans to be consistent. They believe in sauces but all are a variant of the tomato mixed with high explosive. Barbecue is an honorable sauce with its own regulatory agency attached. You know more or less what you're getting into when a rack of ribs is smeared with what looks like nuclear flesh burn. A sauce, half tomato, half black powder. That's fair. The French will not so restrict themselves.

A friend cooked supper one night. He had seen a nice length of walleye I took from the river. "I'll make supper," he said. My friend was born in northern Wisconsin, his uncle was the sheriff of Taylor County when moonshine and bordellos were the principle by-products of reforestation. My friend spent his youth in deer camps and lumber camps, and I trusted him with my fish. He slimed it with a French sauce and it might as well have been cardboard or carp.

The French have not yet visited their politics on corn on the cob. I have no doubt some will yet create a buttery oyster sauce for corn on the cob, or toast that vegetation in red wine. Why the French aren't men enough to drink the wine and leave the food alone I don't know. Some ancestral French gene does not trust food in its natural flavor. Means they haven't been minding their rivers very well if you ask me. If the world ever goes entirely radioactive the French will have the appropriate methods to deal with contaminated cuisine. Same with lifeboat fare or any other catastrophe, where you might end up eating late Aunt Hilda. A sauce at this juncture can be very important. Masking the original context is a good idea. The French are prepared. Why they have to keep experimenting with perfectly good food is beyond me.

Corn on the cob is the only food besides asparagus that is worth poaching. OK, so apples are too. Unknown to most people is the fact that field corn is just as good as sweet corn, with one minor exception. It must be picked at the precise and exact moment of readiness—ten minutes either way is significant. As a kid roused to life in the rule of farmscape, I was a specialized student of corn. I knew it by cribs, feedmills, silos, kerneled, and whole. I knew countryside in those great vintage years when cement stave silos were filled with chopped corn and the smell of ferment permeated every glen and closet in the township. It was a time of the year when a brewery worker and ditch drunk never quite came to, the air was so full of fermentation.

All this knowledge of corn had one principle object, to know when field corn was ripe for corn on the cob. When there were thousands of acres of corn to choose from, a hundred fields to filch. This was the supremest moment of tenting as I remember. To go to the woods the weekend the corn was perfect. Taking along such a minimum of supplies as'd make a Frenchman queasy; nothing else but salt, butter, a shirt pocket of kitchen matches and a Boy Scout canteen. A night in late summer when the moon was full and we off, less as Boy Scouts than as foragers for Mister Grant's Army. No more tent than a hemlock bough, no draught but branch water, and around us ten thousand hectares, more or less, of corn on the cob at the exact, precise, delirious second of succulence.

Being ill-provisioned was in part the lesson. We'd scour the farm junkpiles for buckets, hub caps, tubs in which to boil our ear corn. It meant a wide circle drawn from swamp edge to farm clearing to gain some found object, hollow log, culvert, carboy, silo pipe, oil barrel, or crankcase to boil sweet corn. Crankcases from old trucks were excellent. We returned for wrenches, this caused curiosity and some alarm. Teardrop headlights worked also and gas tanks cut open with our knives.

By now the moon had come, a full and mellow pageant on the horizon. And we, having our camp, went for corn. Whose field? Whittaker? Simonds? Weller? West? O'Neil? Edwards? Wiggy? Newby? It was a delicious feeling to be thieves and cut-throats in the summer night with corn. Doubters will not suppose corn must be hunted, but it surely must, surely as the venison haunch. To pass without detect of farm dog and chicken yard, to filch corn at its tenderest and make away with it stuffed in our pockets, fore and aft, shirts, pants legs, socks, held under our arms and entire stalks over our shoulders. We were foragers in the wake of the Army of Abolition, we had our divine rights, say yes?

Then to bring this enormous booty to camp, build the fire high, rouse the water and cook the corn. The first was always underdone, well under. Followed then a slathering of butter and salt in pure uninhibited gastronomy. A dozen cobs but aperitif, we felt like a cackle of raccoons, cobs thrown every which way, no modern camper knows the like. We were not unkempt, freebooters have no requirement of decorum as envisioned by the Boy Scout Manual. Besides, our shirt tails were untucked.

We ate until our stomachs refused to participate and then somewhere in the middle darkness fell asleep amid a pile of corn stalk and husk. Sleeping the dreams of the toxemic.

In the morning we woke and were appalled at the scene, the wasteland of cob. None asked for breakfast so we left for home and for a week after behaved mannerly, less hungry than before, and smiled a meek no thank you at the invitation to another cob of corn.

Pickups

The pickup truck and agriculture are symbiotic, same as the dog and the flea. Outlaw the tractor and farmers will survive, flatten the shed, no one needs center pivots, potash, urea, lightning rods, jumper cables, milking machines…but don't mess with the pickup truck. Which is why farmers believe God invented the pickup.

Most people don't know God built the first truck; he did. A pickup was idling under a boxelder when Adam stepped out of the mud wondering after his belly button. The first pickup truck didn't have one either.

Was on the fifth day God made the pickup, about four o'clock in the afternoon of a day creating whales, sandhill cranes, badgers. God by this time was bored silly, making animals is awful repetitive since they're all the same, this when God did the truck. The first truck was a jackass, an amiable jackass but still a jackass. What made the jackass a truck was its amiability; womankind and children were the second and third pickup trucks but they weren't made yet.

Adam used the pickup truck to haul firewood on account the Garden got nippy at night and Adam didn't know he was naked though he did know he was cold. Eve was naked as a noodle too but Adam wasn't inclined to tell her and spoil a good thing. God being male had similar thoughts.

The first pickup took more than its fair share of abuse, setting the pattern for trucks ever since. Some western municipalities actually have checkpoints to prevent farm trucks from entry until they've been hosed down and deloused. No farm truck worth its tires is ever washed, a pickup don't see any sin in dirt.

Few years back, anyone who wanted could buy farm plates for their truck; the State Patrol took umbrage at the illicit use of cheap plates and commenced remedial action. People had to prove they were honest farmers, not just gardening maniacs. A clean pickup wearing farm plates was tantamount to a confession and the bears had crime by the nose hair.

Worse thing a farmer can do to a pickup is wash it. When the bank sends the hit-man, a clean truck is no defense. Banks no longer foreclose on farmers, takes too long and auction sales don't educate farmers nearly fast enough. They hire retired IRA bombers with job experience in plastic and remote control. A wad the size of a tobacco plug under the seat cushion is enough to blow the offender off the property, less it's an unwashed and sedimentary truck with six inches of mud and corn cobs.

The very same detonation as to scatter eye teeth from a Mercedes Benz won't no more than sting the farmer's hands. An honest farm truck is a mobile bomb shelter largely immune to high-grade foreclosure.

Before pickups both farmers and jackasses died young, from over-burden, near misses, and a terrible lot of chasing around. A tool here, a tool there, that's what killed farmers. Why they didn't leave the tools in one dash-blessed place is unknown, as a consequence they had to chase tools as often as cows.

What farmers needed was a chance to graze, same as other management types. The reader surely knows that the office desk is less a work instrument than a grazing permit. It resembles well enough an honest workplace but what the desk really affords is the chance to chew the cud. The pickup saved farmers from a certain and horrible fate, in a truck a man can graze yet retain all the appearances of work and tending fields. In truth the farmer is a lot closer to the lotus position than actual labor.

The pickup truck is to agriculture what the ice shanty is to hard-water fishing. You can fish with a plain hole same as you can farm without a pickup truck but the difference is darn remarkable.

What separates a farm truck from an imposter is not only mud enough underneath to build an asteroid, oats sprouting in the box, or the radio tuned to country western. A real farm truck has scars, wounds that come from hauling a ton and a half of high protein on a half-ton rating. From going crosswise the new plowed field pulling a loaded hay wagon. The truck bed looks like a grenade testing range. The toolbox has one of everything from the Sears Roebuck circular, if not what the farmer needs at the moment.

Pickup trucks arrive from the factory complete with a farm-dog, a dog so vital to agriculture it is more likely to see a person riding in back than the dog. Such a truck is not prone to theft, foreclosure, or the IRA so long as the dog is in place. Traffic cops don't much care for dog-occupied trucks either, which is why busted up taillights linger on farm trucks.

Truck manufacturers generally do not understand agriculture. They continue to sell shiny, chrome-plated models with rubber bedliners and velour seats. This puts agriculture off: such a truck though comfortable as a premium coffin is not the right container 'cause it's overdone. An enterprising dealer runs double-aught sandpaper over the finish and drags a file crosswise of the hood, marring the finish as an oak branch would. They let something die and steep in the cab awhile and smear the contents of a grease tube over the engine. Throw away the spare. Cache some Milk Duds and water-logged *Reader's Digests* under the seat, pack the defroster vents full of kitchen matches, the resulting truck sells like hot cakes at an Eskimo convention.

Someday agriculture intends to erect a Hall of Fame of the farmer kind. Early inductees will be Homer MacIntosh the inventor of the toothpick, Chief Oshkosh inventor of bib overalls, John Deere early promoter of green enamel, Skyllar Whittaker barn builder and cuss word artist. Between Cyrus McCormick and Bovine Growth Hormone will reside the statues of farmdog and pickup truck, the dog—done in bronze—will stink some and the truck in blue granite, leaking oil. For once art will have it right.

Land in d minor

Grandpa's land, this is November and I am discing. The potato grading season ended a week previous and I have been discing for a week. The corn-potato rotation requires multiple discing to enhance stalk decomposition. What the land husband wants here is rot and lots of it. Rot sounds uncharitable and vaguely unchristian and contrary to ethical hygiene; I assure you rot is what I want.

Corn stalks are resistant to rot and who can blame them. Farmers worry about corn going slack-kneed before harvest, corn gone weak in the ankles before the picking and the cob lost on the ground where combines can't stoop. As soon as the cob is off and the combine has passed, the stalk can not be wished toward rot quick enough. Farmers switch parties often. Come middle spring we'll all have joined the non-rot party again and signed all the stout stalk petitions then circulating.

Discing is entirely different from other farmwork. There's no crew to hustle, no time haste, no phone calls, no sales to juggle, no delivery trucks to wait out and load or unload. Discing is one of the more premier rites of ag culture whose sense of opulence and kingliness is not diminished by the use of the biggest tractor on the place.

I've said nasty things about modern agriculture, about big tractors going off into a psychosis and indebtedness. I amend all that;
big tractors in November are luminous thrones. If you don't feel
uplifted, dignified, and enthroned in one of these wheeled castles
you ain't got no soul. The particular specimen of my divination
this day is a JD 4840, 200 hp and sixteen thousand pounds of
wheels, green enamel, and cast iron.

I'm enchanted by the way this throne room starts on a cool
morning. I'm sure you're aware that diesels fire the same way
stars do, under the auspices of compression alone. This as you
might guess requires a rigid implementation of mechanical shove.
On a cool morning this tends to leave a battery out of breath. Even
if the John Deere has a pair of them weighing the equal of a compact car. Diesel tractors, particularly the sort that just might qualify as throne room, require finesse in starting. What you have to
work with is the starter key, the throttle setting, and the ether button, these and the exact knowledge the batteries are good for about
six good turns of a cold engine before dying.

All of this can be avoided by using the engine heater. A fif-
teen-hundred-watt heater softens big diesel engines, thins the oil
and enthuses the electrolyte; the tractor with a fifteen-hundred-
watt heater plugged in turns over with the merry abandon of July.
Any fool can start a warm diesel; it takes a special fool to start a
cold diesel in the pedigree of an eight bottom plow.

I have every reason to think other farmers are like me and don't
plug in their throne room tractors on a cold morning because they
want to test whether they are any good at the three-finger ballet
between the starter switch, the throttle setting, and the ether button.

The way a big diesel starts is thrilling, same sort of eager thrill
I get with WWII movies and Spitfires with Allison engines kicked
over and roused to life. Copious cumuli of black smoke, distended
fire, sounds of pistons out of joint, and barely contained explo-
sions. Engine starting, especially dog-hair breathing engines, is a

testosterone boost to every male. Engines are war and firecrackers and rocketry all in one with you sitting on top of the thing. I suspect this doesn't tempt most females.

Discing Grandpa's is quite else from discing the sand side; sand undulates but Grandpa's land has swoop. What the English call swallow. This land oscillates, rises and falls. Off to the south where Valley Up meets Valley Over, the land drops over the edge of the hill and you can see County Trunk J snaking off in the direction of Almond. The road winding into the country is lovely. Discing long fields gives a man the chance to find loveliness in ordinary junk like town road sneaking off to Almond. A person begins to think land has something to do with art. That what art is, what beauty is, ain't straight, ain't linear, but crooked and liable to be stony and don't start easy on cold mornings.

What I got in Grandpa's land is art and to sit on the throne of a big tractor and tend corn stalks toward rot and just look at the land. If this land is music, the key is d minor, a bit mournful but easy to sing out of the middle of your throat and coincidentally the same key as a 200 hp diesel at 2,000 rpm, fifth gear, and a twenty-two-foot disc.

Eckels' Bridge

As a bairn I remember believing in heaven. Must have been the most of twenty minutes, then the salesman mentioned heaven didn't allow dogs, barn cats, garter snakes, milch cows, Morgans or Percherons or Clydes, and neither Allis Chalmers tractors or trees or trout and absolutely no corn silk. I was cured of my want of heaven, least the ointment sold from the pulpit of the Liberty Corners kirk.

Still I realized no matter where in the pew of cynicism a person sets they need a sort of heaven to get them through the lousy chores of life—stone picking, oat bagging and other forms of immoral punishment.

Heaven as I recall beckoned in the prospect of a five-day work week and something resembling an eight-hour day for my Pa, and maybe a cement basketball court and an oil furnace. I dreamed of a land with an oil furnace in every house that grew to fire without expeditions into the January hindlands with wet gloves and ill-starting tractors and so much of my lifetime spent stacking firewood I knew hell had nothing to do with a soul sent to blazes. Hell was hell 'cause somebody had to tend the woodpile of all that inferno. To my thinking hibernation woulda been a lot better invention than indoor plumbing.

The township did have one thing that came so close to heaven I could feel wing nubs sprouting on my shoulder blades. This one adjustment to the penitential shades for the farmkid was Eckels' bridge.

Eckels' bridge was a curious thing, which is what heavens must be. Its irreality combined with its uselessness supported the thought that maybe Eckels' bridge weren't real at all but what happens to folks' minds when deprived of an eight-hour work day.

Built in the manner of timber bridges from the salvage of a preexisting railroad bridge it was black and on hot days sweat out beads of creosote hard as marbles. The bridge was three hundred times the capacity necessary for what traffic wanted to cross the Buena Vista at the low end of Eckels' field.

The real peculiar thing about Eckels' bridge was it didn't go anywhere. A farm lane came over from Eckels' pond and served the field and was deliberate about the task the way farm lanes are. Nice dirt road with no affection for anything in a hurry, the lane came up to Eckels' bridge, crossed it, then flat dab stopped. Beyond the bridge was as bad an insurrection of low woods as a marsh ever had, an indecipherable tangle of hemlock, birch, witch hazel, and piss elm. It was obvious to any who saw it Eckels' bridge wasn't some discarded antique, the woods having grown over the road in an unattended moment. That woods on the lorn side of the creek had never known the touch of a road, from the appearance, not even a logging trail. Nothing more than deer trail and rabbit run; Eckels' bridge never *had* gone anywhere.

As a kid I couldn't be bothered by such obvious transgressions of logic. To my thinking a road going to a bridge then stopping in the middle of its most elegant stride was reasonable enough. I have since learned the ways of the world and see now what the world means when it says a bridge going nowhere is irrational. During my tenure as a kid, Eckels' bridge didn't bother me, I could lie on those cool beams for hours on Sunday afternoons, a bridge that had once served sixteen-wheel locomotives and ninety-six car trains of Union Regiments. Going nowhere seemed entirely reasonable to me those afternoons and to what I knew about the Civil War.

Pa said John Eckels done it, John Eckels being the once under-sheriff of Portage County, the same who saw Joseph Baker shot dead out on the Stockton prairie. Eckels who built the bridge going nowhere.

Still Eckels' bridge did go somewhere and I knew it and every Sunday afternoon worth living knew it. Eckels' bridge weren't intended for regular transport but what is the necessary crossing after common transport was taken care of. Where Eckels' bridge went and went direct was trout and John Eckels built it. Went to a temptation of water that stayed cool despite July and August going to the dogs. Under Eckels' bridge on a hot afternoon were trout all out of proportion to reason. Hundreds, maybe thousands of trout, trout of every size luxuriating in the current between the square beams of Eckels' bridge, the hole it created forty feet deep and all of it stacked with trout.

Nothing was more satisfying than an afternoon on a day so hot it'd blister a tombstone, lying flat on your belly turning creosote-brown yourself and watching trout. Never even thought of fishing from Eckels' bridge, woulda been a sacrilege like smoking cigars in church. We fished trout every other, every cut bank and log trap but not Eckels' bridge. I don't know why. Just weren't right somehow.

The best venture from Eckels' bridge was to stow your clothes in a timber brace and jump the gap. Took a real smoker of a July to try what with the creek just above freezing and white boys looking dangerously like a baited hook, if you know what I mean. To splash down among those trout was the most delivering refresh-ment, and feel trout rub their cold souls against you, the water so cold your muscles froze.

Eckels' bridge burned in the woods fire of '58, burned with a black pall that smelt the whole township of creosote. I have come to think a bridge going nowhere is the exact reference of heaven and why heaven exists. A creosote bridge going nowhere except cold water when you need it most.

The Knotter

J esus Christ never baled hay, if he had he never would have
    been Jesus Christ.
        From a distance, haying sounds religious, all the Jesus
Christs, Mother of Gods, and other devotional phrases rising from
the field in a steady volume of blessed unction.

For the urban pilgrim the source of this volume is not readily
understood, given the technical improvements to haying what with
cannon-balers and green chopping. All agriculture is fair and modern enough with the exception of one machine, and this the cause
of more rude vocabulary, more calling of names, more insulted
heritage, torn hair, thrown wrenches if not outright dare of God to
do his goshdarn awfulest and bring forth the apocalypse. This
skeptic machine produced by the masters of dementia and disillu-
sion?...the square jowled baler of Messrs. John Deere, Interna-
tional Havester and New Idea. Here was a machine said to end the
old awfulness of round bales—round bales as had to be picked
from the ground—and whose mechanical act tis reminiscent of a
rock dove fertilizing a ridge row. Round balers were uncouth the
way they "laid bales." The square baler was to improve this the
brochures said, "bale and load in one smooth operation." "Avoid
delay in the field," "improve forage quality," " a simple machine

49

any fool can repair."

The law could have gotten them on that. All those square baler companies brought to justice for the remark "simple to repair." It is doubtful now that a full generation has passed and is giving off aromatic gases that one farmer in a hundred can honestly attest to ever figuring out the truth of the square baler's knotter. The entire machine was based on this wicked connivance, a thing bewitched with stubby sorts of steel prodded by other bits to whirl around, bow and curtsy, chant a green enamel prayer and produce...a knot. What farmer has not studied and looked, studied and gazed and in six hundred years still does not understand how that knotter works, a most mischievous device. When it ceased functioning there was no certainty of its repair. The knotter on a square baler had to be offered sacrifice and devotion, which is why "Jesus Christ" was so often heard from the hay meadow. The unknowing spectator might think it wrath and sacrilege when instead it was provisioning the knotter with well-being and congratulation, which no knotter can go without.

Some farmers were so trepidatious before the square baler they sent their offspring to various institutions and seminaries for college degrees, and doctorates of law, tithing the family in every direction to understand the workings of a John Deere Model 14T hemp cord knotter. A grandfather took another perspective and accused Deere and Company of pact-making. Any company as would publish on the world a device taking two ends of common twine and in a blink of a mosquito's conscience attach the two ends in one fluid and impermeable knot was guilty of witchcraft. This same grandfather would not approach a square baler without a length of rowan branch in his hand and a Catholic crucifix in his pocket and him only a Methodist of irregular attendance. Obvious to him neither he nor any farmer could repair the thing. If broke it was to be more invocated and supplicated than repaired; an offering of first born was more likely to fix it than a crescent wrench.

My father hired Harry Precourt to drive our hay bailer. He figured we wouldn't kill Harry when the knotter quit. He was right,
we couldn't kill Harry for lousing up the baler 'cause Harry was
married to Esther who was in charge of most of Buena Vista and
the half of Plover our cousin didn't want. So we couldn't kill
Harry when the baler stopped functioning, which is a bad time for
caution when you sure feel like killing something and in goodly
quantities if only so the knotter feels better. Pa knew if he had
entrusted baling to any combination of the family members someone wasn't gonna survive the day, knotters being what they are;
besides brothers are prone to kill each other for lesser causes than
the John Deere knotter.

The only woman I ever bit drove a hay baler. She was responsible for the baler's discontent as any country person can tell you.
The person on the hay rack is responsible for the load and its
proper grip on the hay rack, knowing as I'm sure you do a load of
hay must grip the rack not merely loiter on it. So the driver then is
in charge of the baler.

I hit my wife when we were baling marsh hay. The knotter had
quit for the six millionth time and she'd jarred the load loose in at
least forty badger holes. She thinking if the tractor missed the badger diggings the rest of the machine ought too, when any nincom-
poop knows a tractor, hay baler, and wagon are all flying separate
formations and if you miss a badger hole with one the odds are
you'll hit it with the next. All this is John Deere's designed method
of improving the species by raising the likelihood of homicide.
When John Deere sets out to improve agriculture they mean to do
so even it if it takes murder to do it. This the same reason they put
four hundred times the chains and bevel gears on any one machine
than mere function requires, to eliminate the foolish, like those
who try to slide a chain on without throwing in the PTO clutch.
And, generally, this has improved agriculture. At least there are
fewer folks willing to agricult than there used to be, including the

few million driven mad by the knotter and those killed off by mechanical digestion.

Once you get through to this theory of elimination in agriculture you're probably all right. You might have to hit the wife to get the knotter going but that's better than killing off the kid. Besides, if you kill the kid how you gonna fix it next time?

Dandelion Wine

Wine, the opening verse in wine, women and song, had in the community of my origin a low station. The prophesy being the merest draft of this liquid spook could unhinge the otherwise sober and sane and send them off in a fit of sexual congress and musicology. To legend proofs were added. Victims were quietly pointed out whom wine had corrupted and stalled on their way to proficiency. Suffering now their fates: ill-fitting marriage, hired-manism, game-law villainy, or barns of the unpainted kind.

The Christian lands in the nestle of Valley Up, Valley Down, and Valley Over was done in a manner following the original John Wesley patent. To whit the kirk at the juncture of the county roads invited universal and holy communion with grape juice. A tangy and resplendent purple, served in tiny glasses along with crumbs of Mrs. Eckels' white bread.

As a kid I did not understand the poetic interpretation of this Holy Relic. Communion seemed a churlish event, given this was the very same God as had chased off the mournfulness of winter by inventing Christmas and announced spring to the northern hemisphere by the resurrection of every dead seed and root. If Christianity extended the charity and the power of the flower to a

like and luxurious practice on the human soul, I did not understand how it was methodees had not also transcended the supper
table. They had all the makings for divine ecstasy. Needed was not
a lick in the glass of Welch's grape juice but a smear of rambunc-
tious blackberry jam on a slice of Mrs. Eckels' whole wheat and
this sufficient to win the reluctant heart from sin. Even a well-
done apple pie woulda done it, or peach cobbler, or a warm sacri-
ficial doughnut for whose likes Grandma Fletcher was famous. Do
this in remembrance of the wood-tink of Nazareth and it'd be
standing room only at the kirk. Both barrels loaded and primed
every Sabbath, not just Easter and Christmas. Blackberry jam and
newborn bread woulda routed sin like a gale sends leaves. Instead
it was grape juice, watery, loose moraled grape juice.

The problem for my farm town was that wine and sin were
indistinguishable one from the other, according to John Wesley,
mutual travelers on the same narrow path, apparently without
reverse gear, headed straight for damnation. To find the practice of
winemaking in this cautious farmship was one of the miracles of
humankind. The agent for its promotion was a standard agricultural practice easily amended to the original Ten Commandments.
This supreme ordinance was none other than the Noxious Weed
Law posted on the Town Hall door the first Wednesday of May
forewarning citizens to mind their herbicides else the town would
at the owner's expense. And everyone knew the town crew was
paid hourly and not by piecework, god bless 'em.

If a test is one day perfected to assay the IQ of biology, the
dandelion will emerge supreme. No other plant in all of bounding
nature is so wise, so conniving, and practices such marked
vengeance on the human race. None else has the unrestrained wit
and territorial ambitions of dandelions. As a child my life was corrupted in exact proportion to the extent that dandelions ruled the
field and pasture. The spring of my existence was spent in pursuit
of every sign and indicator of that root. Every tactic was followed

for the removal of that plant whether by poison or dissolution; ashes, cow pee, drain oil and creosote. I picked, hoed, chopped, shoveled, spat, fumigated, plowed, harrowed, pummeled, stoned and stomped, I burned tires and oak branches over the spot where dandelions were last seen. All without effect. Dandelions grew and bloomed through every fortification and chain armor devised.

Dandelion wine began with weed control. Any wine as gained conformance to the Noxious Weed Law had the approval of the Town Board. And any weed as might be turned into wine was considered an honest practice of agriculture.

The favored object in this was dandelion wine as practiced by Jesse Whitcom Riley Grant, Township of Plover.

Jesse was as chilled by temperance as his fellow parishioners, only venturing beyond its strictures to maintain his duty to agriculture and eradication. Any method known to displace dandelions from the field was in accord with Divine Opinion. Which might lead one to think harlotry might have gained practical employment if found beneficial to the field or adding companionship to the plough. Such a connection was never made and commercial harlotry died out in the river city when the loggers left town but wine survived through the diligence of Jesse Grant.

Jesse was fossil related to the Grants in remote Scotland who distilled another sort of wine, baptized after the place of its birth with the name Glenfiddich. This was an agricultural solution to an over supply of barley that left to its own might attract mice, also in surplus. If it hadn't been for agriculture, the business of luminous fluids might have ended with John Wesley's injunction.

Jesse Grant sold vegetables and strawberries at a roadside stand, a comfortable enterprise that preyed on tourists and villagers mostly, who paid ridiculous prices for sweet corn just to satisfy themselves with association with a moonshiner of local legend. They bought choice specimens of blueberries, hubbard squash. Was Jesse who introduced zucchini into the locality before it too became a weed. His art was sweet corn ripe by the Fourth of July, same arrival time for new potatoes and peas, and of course strawberries, tidy pints of intoxicating fruit in basswood baskets. On the back wall of the shop was a small, hand-lettered sign reading "Dandelion Wine, sample or container." T'was to this came the worshipful pilgrimage. All those knotted up in the bindweed of Methodism, chill Water Dunkers, and Synod Loots, who were enjoined from alcohol but might do what they could for weed control.

Grant's Famous Tonic cured the mournfulness and penitential shades that haunted those somber decades when farms were hand dug from the stumplands of the Wisconsin Pinery. Since the bottle was as much feared as the contents, dandelion wine came in measures to deflect suspicion, mason jars mostly, pints and quarts in blue glass, milk bottles, horse liniment jars, cough syrup and catsup bottles. For one hypersensitive matron of the church, dandelion wine tied in rubber galoshes. She had heard sin and damnation was to be found in the bottle but nary a warning about the eight-buckle overshoe.

It was a pale liquid, if more crystalline and indolent than a liquid ought be. Held up to the window in a glass tumbler, dandelion wine bent light like a lens. It was not the spectrum Isaac Newton endorsed, with far too many colors like those in the super set of Crayolas. A wine to bathe the soul. To touch the core of brown earth ploughmen who might by it behold invisible hues. Its taste became legend. Served in the evening of hay-making in the vacant moment before supper, dandelion wine suspended the farmer in a space between heaven and earth. A less earnest and graceful space. Where stars and dusk mattered more and the number of bales mattered less. It was again a luxury to breathe the country air and let the sweat congeal and day find an end. Jesse's formula put all what was impending and inexplicable to rest. And it was weed control.

Pigs, Chickens
and Rutabagas

L and is a principal tenet of farming. As a consequence clearing land is an act of farming. To those who have served this act it is one of the more disagreeable and hostile honors attached to agriculture. Once all farmers were pilgrims and as such we were brush whackers, this it should be noted in the long long ago before bulldozer, dynamite, and the chainsaw, before even the singular improvement of horse and ox. Clearing land was the most unkind of those specialized terrors facing the farmer. While harvesting and planting and winter wood were odious enough, clearing land had no equal for the enormity of the task. It was one cruelty followed by another, all contrived to make of savage woods some useful citizen.

It was natural given the bruising nature of the obligation that farmers did invent interesting and efficient shortcuts to field-making. On first inspection the edification of a woods is a venerable subject, it looks impossible largely because it is impossible. A mortal looking at the woods knows it never can be done, it is too unequal; all those trees, roots, horrifying briars, the impenetrable thickets, the blood-letting tangles, the venomous vines, those patulous shades. People with their hearts set on clear land were in for a dose of dementia a lot sooner than they were likely to see open

ground. Many left agriculture, choosing vocations with better
chances of survival.

With this in mind it need be remembered farmers are inventive
sons, underneath the grime and gristle of their idiotic profession is
a stubborn hope of finding an easier way of doing awful things.

My grandfathers were the last generation of farmers to suffer
agriculture B.B.D.C., that is before bulldozer, dynamite and chainsaw. They necessarily had to find methods of land clearing without
resorting to B.D.C. or avoid the whole thing and leave the woods
alone, which wasn't very modern or manly. The reader might think
any improvement to land clearing B.B.D.C. was hopeless but such
was not the case because farmers had three allies in land clearing.
Three allies that when deployed on woods reduced it to manage-
able ruin, from whence comes the title of this epistle: pigs, chickens, and rutabagas.

The Indians and our pilgrim forefathers killed a woods by gird-
ing the trees, a good process but time-consuming and spiteful with
mosquitoes and midges being what they are. The improvement of
this method in the time B.B.D.C. was to buy a dozen hogs, confine
their attention to a local woods, and let them modernize it. Without
redress to axe or cross-cut saw, a herd of pigs will reduce the
prospects of a woods quicker than a Swedish double-bit and never
once having to mind them from the spring day they were turned out
till winter. After one summer of pigs a woods is already dying. At
two years of pigs a woods is cut to half its original population and
the undergrowth is gone completely. After three years not a patch
of grass remains and only the hardiest species remain, the rest have
died, dropped their limbs and await the woodcutter's saw.

Some farmers with the same objective in mind preferred
chickens to pigs, the benefit is the added height of defoliation.
Pigs will kick the daylights out of a woods, kill trees, uproot and
slaughter, but pigs have a hard time getting any altitude. Chickens,
who were ordained by God for this purpose on account they were

denied real flight, will climb a tree and chew the bejesus out of it as high up as a tree cares to go. During the night chickens roost in the branches and defile everything below, making a chicken woods after a rain squall about the greasiest place on earth to venture save a shopping mall on the day after Thanksgiving. Whether chickens or pigs kill off a woods more efficiently is unknown.

The last land clearing implement available B.B.D.C. was the rutabaga. Little is known of the origin of this vegetation. Some have offered that it is a species of pig as never made it all the way to pig, having a body contour quite obvious of pig, meaning squat, round, and ridiculously colored.

My grandfathers employed rutabagas, usually in the second year of the pig rotation. Seeding a woodlot with rutabagas pretty much finished off the woods. The reader will please understand pigs have an affection for the rutabaga, they will dig for it, they will conduct tunnels, fashion burrows, and install subways, sewers, and cellars of eager diggings to get at rutabagas. As a consequence the wood is not only denuded but felled. A second dose of rutabagas and pigs will smash up a woods into stovewood lengths, if a little haphazard in the pile.

By the fourth year the former woods was ready to plant to corn, assuming the pigs had been killed off. A living pig can not, nor will not, be kept from a rutabaga woods and must be put to death if the cornfield is to enjoy safe keeping. The rutabaga attraction is so durable and ingrained in the hope of pigs they will ruin a cornfield looking for rutabagas, and this a hundred generations since the last pig and last rutabaga met in the woods.

Apple Earth

In the spring of 1885 Vincent Van Gogh painted what's known as the "Potato Eaters." The scene depicts a family at the evening meal of potatoes. The lamp over the table clearly illumines the faces and profiles of those seated. The painting grasps a spiritual calm, of working people, of common laborers and farmers taking supper.

"Potato Eaters" is a transcendence of earlier renditions of the Nativity. The same light, the earnest faces, and the gathering to celebrate an otherwise ignorable event, a supper of potatoes.

Whether Vincent Van Gogh intended "Potato Eaters" to be compared with the religious paintings of Raphael or Rembrandt is for art historians to decide. What he did capture in "Potato Eaters" one hundred years ago is the durable relationship between the farmer and the potato.

The potato had come a long way to be painted by a master a short three years before his death. As a farmer, a potato farmer, I take pleasure at the earth reverence captured by Vincent Van Gogh. The spirit of a family, as caught in the elegance of the woman's face in the center of the painting. Van Gogh's sacrilege is to put such a countenance on a peasant, transforming what is holy at the Nativity to the supper table, exchanging the Christ Child for boiled potatoes.

Like many artists Vincent Van Gogh was a precarious genius. The tortured aspects of his life impugn his sanity. This occurrence in art is too common for coincidence. Art transcending the narrow confines of madness. It was Van Gogh who saw light in bundles, what Max Planck the physicist later described as quanta. The profundity is of humanity escaping its condition, whether of madness, inconsequence and poverty, or ignorance.

The peasant and the potato were synonymous in the late seventeenth and eighteenth centuries. Discovered during Pizarro's conquest of the Incas by a starving corps of conquistadors, the accident occurred in the village of Sorocota, as chronicled by Jean Castellano: "Here at least we found their means of sustenance, a roasted nut of wonderful size and flavor buried in the ashes of the campfires." The world had discovered the baked potato.

Most agricultural practices of the New World people were superior to those of Europe. The basis for this judgement is the adaptive range of plants Native Americans developed from wild settings to cultivated crops. The Americas, in simple terms, had a dietary base many times more complex than that of Eurasia.

At the time of Pizarro the Incas had developed standard practices of crop rotation, irrigation, short and long term storage, and something amazing to even modern agriculture, controlled production.

The potato returned to Spain in the robes of the padres. The study of plant science was at the time almost completely in the hands of monasteries, where monks across Europe toyed with varietal experiments. It was no accident Prior Gregor Mendel wrote the first elementary text on genetics.

From Spain the potato found its way again to the New World and to the colonies at St. Augustine. Francis Drake after plundering the Spanish Main in 1568 picked up Walter Raleigh's failing colony on Roanoke. Whether Raleigh obtained the potato through barter or Drake "borrowed" them of the Spanish is not known. Raleigh, an avid plant experimenter, returned them to his Ireland estate. During the next fifty years the "Virginia potato" gradually gained favor. Of the potato it was said that a family of six might sustain themselves with a two-acre patch. Official steps were taken encouraging the use of the "Irish potato" in Britain and the colonies.

Except for the Irish, the Empire seemed reluctant to take on the potato with any enthusiasm. The Scots went so far as to reply "good Presbyterians would plant none of the heathenish food recommended by Papist neighbors." The problem of acceptance lay with the potato's membership in the nightshade family, the plant implicated during the witch trials as the "Devil's herb." The potato vine does have narcotic properties, scopolamine is found in all parts of the nightshade group, chiefly in the flowers and leaves. American Indians used a relative, jimson weed, to initiate novices into the spirit world. Heavy doses of scopolamine promote frightening hallucinations populated by monsters, devils, and frenzy. Modern uses include sleeping pills, remedy for the runny nose and allergies. Once it was used widely during childbirth as an amnesic, the mother often having no recall of the birth experience.

The potato was viewed throughout most of Europe with suspicion. It took the French and Louis XVI to establish social acceptance for the potato. Benjamin Franklin was present with other diplomats at an all-potato dinner. Marie Antoinette appeared with a potato flower in her hair, and all the dishes served from the hors d'oeuvres to soup and entrée were potatoes. The story is told of how Louis had a potato field planted on the main road to the peasant market. A shift of guards kept the curious from the field until the crop ripened, then the night sentry was withdrawn. Pilferage took its natural course and the potato found its way into French cuisine.

By the early 1800s, the potato was the peasant food of Eurasia. It fed the family and the cattle alike. From Ireland to Russia, Holland to France, Poland to Spain, the potato became universally identified as the food of the peasantry.

Van Gogh's life seemed a perpetual wandering. His anguish

followed him in his activities and his moods. During the winter of 1879 he ministered to the coal miners of Belgium. From there he wrote to his brother Theo he was "attending free courses at the great university of misery."

Van Gogh painted three different versions of "Potato Eaters." The first is somber, the background indistinct, the only sustenance is the plate of potatoes in front of four adults and a child. In a third version Van Gogh has raised the spiritual energy. The room is broadly illuminated. The subjects are no longer subdued by poverty. The clock on the wall now has a recognizable movement. The faces of the characters are not glazed over, the figures are looking at each other. The brown of their labor and place mixed equally with the tone of their innate humanity. They are enduring persons. The central woman figure has not lost her femininity to the brutishness of rustic life. Van Gogh imparts a moment to the scene, the plate of potatoes around which they are gathered seems to glow.

One hundred years ago Vincent Van Gogh painted potato farmers taking supper, at first seeing only the cruelty of fate and ceaseless labor, then moving beyond to humanness preserved if not exalted. "Potato Eaters" is earth made holy.

Night Plowing

We heard him plowing. Had to listen for him between peepers offering bids on the whole countryside and diesel trucks on the state road. You wouldn't think frogs to be so overt in hill land or know Valley Over is the spring head of the Buena Vista Creek. Twenty-five miles west they've got an eighteen-hole gopher course on it and a nightclub with French menus. Same creek as starts in Valley Over runs by that restaurant but they can't call it a creek so it's a river; some kind of natural sequence is involved.

Frogs are the company in early spring. We heard their sound slide over the rim from Valley Over to Valley Up. Could hear frogs all the way to Berry's honey hill and past Fletcher's curve in the Valley Down.

We were talking potato prices before we heard the peepers and how it didn't look good what with Delaware and Jersey late and the Maine crop up. Means heck for the eastern market. Besides, Alabama and Carolina are slow to ground, so the southern market will be awful loose-jointed too. It helps to know aforehand how much you might miss by so to deflate your anticipation. A farmer can almost feel good if only knowing a little beforehand what cheap is and not have the wind come on him sudden and all the barn doors open.

The peepers ruined our discourse. My mind went off in a frog direction and I had to ask him to say whatever it was over again. He did and I missed it the second time. We gave up on potatoes and leisured in peepers. He turned thirty-five yesterday and we were there celebrating at his house with lasagne and birthday cake. Afterward he and I sat on the porch venting cigars, hearing peepers, talking prices, and Seguin Peters night plowing.

Seguin Peters has no reason to plow. He retired from farming ten years ago so we wondered why he was sneaking three bottoms out in a dilute mix of night and spring.

Was two years ago when from the back porch and another spring birthday we watched IRAS-Araki-Alcock come within two million, nine hundred thousand miles. That's close for interplanetaries, particularly if you consider it started out half-way between here and Centaurus, about twelve trillion miles off the south end of the porch.

Found IRAS-Araki-Alcock off the point stars of the big dipper named Dubhe and Merak. Seen the night previous south of there, more towards Thuban. The old Saxons thought of the Big Dipper as a plow. When it's swung over in the spring night they hold it is time to turn ground. The Big Dipper does look like a plow if you know a plow is mostly mold-board and beam.

We figured Seguin Peters must have missed plowing. Hill country and its sensational kind of night plowing. The prerequisites are stony land, a dose of early night, and a plow. Some folks who have farmed forever have never seen it 'cause they can't get over the notion they have to steer. Which generally is true except for plowing when the front wheel tracks the lead furrow. Plow tractors don't need steering any more than ARAS-Araki-Alcock needs steering. Once situated a man can stay comfortable for eighty rods. Turn the lights off and let the tractor steer its own self by stars and the dark furrow. Which is when he sees it if he's gonna. The trail of dull sparks burning off the last bottom. A regular tail sometimes. Sparks off feldspar, gneiss, rose quartz, greenstone, sands, chert, granite, and purple flint. A big stone strikes such fire as to lay in the furrow burning in the growl of stone disturbed. If you're turned, you'll see it.

We figured the frogs called Seguin out. Peepers started it. He remembered the feeling of night plowing and wanted it again.

Was almost one o'clock before he quit, which is the spell of hill country plowing and stones set fire. Started out as a garden patch. Went on to a size for sweet corn. Now Seguin has twenty acres plowed. He couldn't get loose of night plowing till the fence stopped him. Long orbits swinging on an old pull.

My Sister's
Driving Lesson

It had been the same with horses. The farmboy learned to drive horses by osmosis, maybe it was intuition but somehow it came, the ability to drive and it seemed as if you always knew. Driving a tractor came the same way, no book, no instruction, like the sorcerer's apprentice we knew without being told.

Girls of course were hopeless. My sister once tried to drive a Ford 8N tractor, which in its time served well enough but now is looked on as a pathetic tractor compared to the sumptuous castles of the modern cult. The neat thing about the 8N was its controls were straightforward. The normal practice among tractor manufacturers confused the function of every control lever and pedal. Besides, they added an extra set of everything, levers that didn't do anything except augment the mechanical grandeur of senatorial tractors.

The problem with girls and anything mechanically lethal is they can not concentrate on the exquisite hazard without thought of their appearance. Females invented the rear view mirror and it had nothing to do with following traffic. Females don't understand tractors. I have never met a penitent tractor in all my life. Men know the mechanical world is divided; some are simple organisms, harmless and harboring no intrigue, the rest are raptors, machines of prey waiting for the operator to do something stupid then chew them off.

Every farmkid who has spent time studying the hands of farmers knows tractors are a terrible commandment. This hungry reputation ought have dampened the ardor of farmboys to drive tractors, it did not. In truth a little requiem music only added to the adventure of tractors and farming in general. Girls never caught on; they were too busy adjusting their faces.

I'm not saying my sister was stupid but she was after all female. Like most females she did not make any distinction between machines of prey and the pitcher pump. She thought if she could drive a Chevrolet surely she could drive a tractor. The assumption may look reasonable but it isn't, the tractor is to an automobile what a sledge hammer is to a tack hammer. A car will go 60 mph but not a whole heck else. Hitch a bale wagon to a car and it loses its peerage, like trying to pound a well point with a tack hammer. Or hang a picture nail with a sledge hammer. A tack hammer miss is not the same regret as a sledge hammer. Sister didn't know this.

On the farmstead the granary sat more or less equidistant from the house and the barn, all farmyards are like this though I don't know why. An alley circled the granary passing in order the gas pump, corn crib, chicken coop, feedmill, and car garage. For years this circuit served as course for every picnic footrace, sack race, and bicycle derby. Here, sister was to demonstrate her skills as a tractor pilot. She who disputed tractor steering was anything more than a transfer of Chevrolet skills. No attempt was made to instruct her error.

She got the thing started because Henry Ford had been plain obvious with the ignition key, and found a gear. Had she noticed the shift pattern stamped indelibly on the transmission her fate might have been softer.

I saw straight off she was in trouble but believed a learning experience might improve her. It was fourth gear, on an 8N equal to 16 mph. A trivial speed. A paltry velocity anywhere, except the granary circuit whose hazard and radius distort the trivial.

When she let out the clutch we knew we were in for a spectacle. First off 'cause she hadn't the foggiest which of a half dozen levers and pedals on the machine had been the clutch, and second, the abrupt launch of the tractor had dislodged her from the seat and she was pinched between the seat proper and the hitch stem. She had to reach for the steering wheel and it woulda been darn awkward for a boy much less a girl at 16 mph.

Girls have a noise unique to them, resembling a war cry of a Confederate infantryman. An octave rendering the scratch of a stainless steel dinner fork on dirty blackboard a pleasant hymn by comparison. The sound can suck the galvanizing off a windmill. This, what sister at the moment was expelling.

Car driving is for sissies as every farmboy knows. Cars have a single pedal and all that is required to rein in the contraption is to mash the thing to the floor and eventually it comes to a halt. Tractors have two brake pedals, one for the right side, one for left. This, so tractors can do what horses did, turn at right angles and fit places mechanical motivations were never intended. To stop a tractor requires judicious application of those two pedals, jamming either one at velocity isn't a good idea. Sister didn't know this.

The tractor did as it was told and took off in another direction, aimed now at the flank of the barn. Happily a door approximate to the tractor's dimensions was placed in this wall, unhappily an equal was not in the opposite wall. Amazing how the female voice carries. Not having learned a whole lot by her first jab at the brakes she gave another, all the while whooping like a crane caught at scandal. As proof the gods watch over girls more than farmboys the tractor headed in a direction oblique of absolute disaster, this time in the heifer barn. Heifers being excitable animals and capable athletes besides took the only recourse open to them and exited the windows. It resembled the abandonment of the

Lusitania. Heifers big-eyed and afraid for their souls hurtling one over the other. Unfortunately the heifer door was closed.

One last shriek exited the late sister, then a collision mixed with miscellaneous sounds of lumber, followed by the most poignant silence the world has ever known. Knowing our sister had been killed off I shook hands with my brothers and went to collect the corpse. Alas, the tractor had taken the brunt of the collision and she was bowed over the wheel sobbing pitifully.

Any farmboy knows when a similar end visits a male, embarrassment alone is enough to kill. If I had accomplished what my sister had I would have been sold to the rendering plant for unscented soap. Sister didn't get sold into slavery, instead Pa hugged her to his overalls, patted the back side of her head and said something doughie. Males wouldn't do this to each other.

Maybe girls can't drive tractors but they can sure steer what counts.

The Painting

The painting hangs over the piano. A brooding, melancholy scene primitively drawn, the elements lie flat as caricature in a child's coloring book. The composition is all wrong, the lighting ridiculous, the background is illuminated while the foreground is heavy shadowed and closed over with a mantle of tangled trees. A running spring in the exact center of the painting is oppressive and uninviting, bearing almost the smell of its squalid site.

I have never cared for that painting. Neither the heavy duty Victorian frame, a turn of the century stone boat containing enough plaster to drywall a small house. The gilt-work is boorish, excessive, and the wood robust enough for fenceposts.

The painting is my wife's fault. It came as part of her dowry tucked in the bottom of the cedar hope chest that dates her romance and anyone old enough to marry her. Her family is old-line Milwaukee, Germanic to the very nostril, bald pate and snoring umlauts. The family participated in all the vital deutschlander stuff like marching bands and Christmas is still conducted as one enormous chocolate-flavored free-for-all. I had to take the painting as part of the deal for marrying the woman. Since, I have questioned the wisdom of getting taken prisoner by the Kaiser Wilhelm types; the painting has hung over the piano the whole while.

I once asked my wife what supposedly is represented in the painting. It was some years before she attempted a reply. She read into my inquiry a condescending sneer, something about the paint being better used to fuel Dante's inferno, she implying I had assailed her forebears, my undue body-language impugning their art sense. As you know I did nothing of the sort. In truth it was an altogether innocent inquiry regarding the intent of the original artist with nothing the least suggestive that the family might suffer imbeciles above the statistical average. Doubtless no fault of their own due to the lead content of the water in that region of Indiana.

Illinois, she said.

I meant Illinois.

Was a picnic spot, she told me eventually. A picnic spot at a great grandma to the third or fourth power's farm somewhere in Illinois.

Didn't look picnicy to me, the scene couldn't have been more somber with a lynch rope hanging from the tree branches. Picnics are sunny, airy, open, like beaches and parks. This scene was so dark that compared to it a black hole would stand out like a brush fire in a tamarack bog. Just looking at the thing gave me a sense of depression and blight.

I do admit I didn't care for the painting. In fact several times I removed it when she wasn't home, set it behind the piano after pulling the wire out from the frame so it looked accidental.

She noticed straight away. All the while looking at me like I got caught red-handed molesting the Pope's maiden aunt.

Once I bought her this enormous oriental porcelain, the kind she is partial to. The thing dwarfed and probably outweighed a cannonball. I filled it with flowers and a mushy Hallmark card. The kind I never get unless I'm in trouble. I put it on the piano.

She loved me for that and acted grateful as heck. This sentiment lasted about a minute and then she turned her lynx eyes on me and burned cosmic rays into my bones. I mean malevolently stared.

You bastard, she said.

There ain't no judicial review on a sentence and banishment like this. I've since left the painting alone. I did hang a Picasso print next to it, hoping to educate my wife. Hoping she'd see real art is superior to great grandma to the fourth somewhere in Illinois. People don't pay good money for Picasso prints for no reason. Maybe she'd notice how Picasso handled the medium with an air of buoyancy, not the ten tons of barn paint employed by great grandma in Illinois.

Years passed. My family has picnics, if not all that many on account of the farm. Once we had a picnic on Lake Superior owing it had rained July fourth and for the two days previous. The rest of the time I had good intentions of a picnic and going to the lake, even promising to have fieldwork done by noon, one o'clock at the latest. Nice Saturday afternoon picnic with her and the kids but we'd leave the dog home 'cause the beach had rules against dogs. About noon the end boom on the irrigation caught a tree branch and attempted a gymnastic last rite. We didn't go picnicking that day. Similar occurrences followed.

She gave up asking.

I think it was that awful hot summer. I was mowing hay Saturday afternoon having had trouble all morning with the hydraulics. Frustrated, I didn't go home for lunch and halfway through the afternoon I was still mad. Lucky if I had the hay down before dark and so blame hot you could cook an egg on the bottom of a rock. I wasn't in the mood to picnic.

'Bout two thirty I saw the pickup truck moving its way down the lane, kids in back, the dog too. I wasn't in much mood for them either. She got out of the truck wearing that spaghetti-strap thing about as transparent as a French kiss. The dress gives me goosebumps. Had a blanket and picnic basket in her arms, I dirtier than sin, oilier than Midland Texas. Didn't seem to matter to her and the rye sandwich tasted fine with a hint of hydraulic oil, the beer even better. Chocolate chip cookies, an apple. I fell asleep.

Woke up to the sound of the kids and dog in the creek. Not much of a swimming hole since the water even at mid-summer is about ten degrees above freezing. From the sound I gathered it didn't matter.

Climbing back on the tractor I looked back at her in the shade by the creek. Next thing I remember was a kind of sob come out of me. The scene was inimical to that of the painting, a dark, melancholy shade, the stream at the center, behind the sunlight fields, except in this scene was my wife and kids and their delight.

The painting it seemed had come off the wall and fit itself to the backside of the farm the same as it had in Illinois, where once were other children making painful noises in the cold water and other wives on the bank wondering if the oil stains will come out of the dress. They didn't go to the beach neither.

I looked up great great great grandma's farm in Illinois, curious to find what the picnic spot looked like now. Close as I can figure it's the parking lot across the road from the steel mill. Union wages, three-day weekends, a week at a resort beach in South Carolina, the kind of vacation every family needs.

I've got a slightly used Picasso print if anybody wants one.

The Spring Drill

Certain farm habits exist as much for their poetic expression as for their utility. The verification of this motive is not at hand. Farmers do not presume themselves or their duties to be poetic, poetry is for musicians, painters, versifiers.

The grain drill is a standard field implement, its purpose to seed oats, rye, alfalfa, clover, and miscellaneous other grasses as follow agriculture. From all aspects a charmless device.

A wide instrument is the grain drill. Even in the golden days of the three-bottom plow the grain drill stood ten feet wide from wheel nut to wheel nut.

A very obvious device is the drill, not the least bashful on the townroad. In fact it hogs the road in a superlative innocence thrilling the farmer's heart. By this act the farmer knows his personal ownership of this earthly place, by this occlusion, this thrombosis, this arterial blockage, the heart-attack and cerebral stroke convened as a wheeled vehicle on the townroad. Here, the farmer knows the joy of the motorcycle gang; all else waits on the passage of the grain drill. The drill then has its moment, a majesty other machines do not experience, but it is not hogging the townroad only that thrills the farmer.

Once upon a time the grain drill was the farm equivalent of the steam calliope, at least when it came to its passage on the town-road. If not completely accurate, the statement is the appropriate sense of malediction and temper to which the grain drill was capa-ble. The innocent must understand the drill. A mischievous machine born out of wedlock, consisting of dissimilar politics, alien chromosomes, unrelated parts, conjoined without authority, all conspiring to noise.

Mounted on top of the drill were seed boxes, into these the grass seed was poured. Two such: one voluminous, the other smaller, the more circumspect one for alfalfa thoughts. Both had covers, that is to say sounding boards. The bins were of straight white ash painted the same coarse, insincere hue as the rest of the drill. Beneath these boxes were nefarious and numerous individual tubes, their purpose to numb the population. Spring steel tubes as wobbled about like a dead snake absolved of its sins. Below these tubes were the sowing discs, two per row, angled to each other to open the seeding vein, made of the same tensile steel as symphony cymbals. Behind were various links of chain whose alleged pur-pose was to cover the seeded row, a fraudulent plot if ever there was one. The entire haberdashery of this was borne on two large, that is to say unstill, steel wheels long after the farmstead had become rubber-tired. A most antique sort of spoke and iron rim as can not be muffled.

Understand seeding oats is the first spring obligation. As soon as the thaw permits is oat-time, frost in the ground doesn't matter. Oats then are the first seeds in the ground, the day as likely to be near blizzard as sunshine. Drilling oats on a day in new April is an old artifice of farmers. Same oats, same ground, same rude kind of spring, if a different farmer, this the same as always. It is a moment too exquisite for words. Porridge and oatmeal begin here. Oat planting is a day so attached, so alloyed to the farmer's id it defies all attempts to exorcise. Here then is where the grain drill gets its wanton attitude to hog the townroad.

The reader will have noted in the grain drill's construction this is an educated machine and not some accidental pretense. The wooden bins, the spring steel tubes, the tensile disks, and the raggle of chains together cause an instrument of orchestral churn followed after by hallelujah havoc. The entirety towed ahind a tractor. On any sort of townroad the drill ringled and jingled. No matter whether gravel or MacAdam, every stone, every cobble taught this instrument to sing. The steel wheels redoubled the verse. The bins hollow as a zither's heart warbled the noise, two different pitches all at once. A grain drill on the townroad had the same zeal and energy as a hundirt and twelve piece orchestra locked up in a closet playing the blind Mister Beethoven's 1812 Overtrump. An unstoppable noise this grain drill, all at one gangling, ringing, gesticulating, defamative, loudable, unrepentant volume. Noise. The countryside dissolved before the grain drill and its noise. Babies cried, women wept, unprotected children wet their pants, such was the trauma and resulting ozone. Those who did not know better believed the great final chapter of Mankind was at hand. The pounding notes tore nails from barn boards, gave birth to frogs out of chicken eggs, soured milk, deafened eardrums, sent a tingle of electrocution through every spine and harried rats from beneath the outhouse. It was an adoration of noise two generations before rock music and 10,000 watts. It loosened false teeth, broke chimney brick, cracked teapots, commenced ovulation, hardened cement, killed bats outright, interfered with radio waves, and otherwise thrilled and titillated every inhabitant on the townroad.

And if there was once a surplus of oats, whose price by the bushel was not worth the loose change in an Irishman's pocket, then the noise of the spring drill on the townroad knew why. Not noise exactly. A tinglement if not honest song, an induction of delight spread along every farmlane and hardroad. A ringing in of spring by those too shy to sing. To haul after the tractor the spring drill was to conduct, or at least invoke from the tractor seat the music-of-the-spheres and eschew all other moral behavior for the purchase of this noise alone. If it hogged the road awhile it did not matter. For it was once believed and fervently so the call and song of the spring drill was what roused the earth again to life and other farm habits.

Tractors

E very farmer sooner or later becomes a tractor nut; usually this is not a voluntary response. The more critical case is the poor sod who attempts to collect tractors, again quite involuntarily. Usually the person in question is not aware he is collecting tractors, however the weed patch behind the machine shed has a swelling population of them. Tractors, all makes, all models, none of which internally combust.

As the reader can well imagine a tractor collection is not the same sweet-mannered hobby as the housewife's penchant for oriental teapots or Hummel figurines. Tractors don't fit the shelf, dusting seems perverted, and you can't even mow around them so the backside of the machine shed soon is infiltrated with weed species that apparently thrive on gear oil, rust, and tire fluid. Burdock and pigweed in this medium grow taller than the Amazon rain forest along with a few boxelders designed by Salvador Dali. Snakes adore such a setting. Mice live and die in every toolbox. It all happens because the farmer kept a tractor too long and it no longer is worth anything for trade. Matter-of-fact the deal is contingent on the farmer keeping the old tractor even though the dealer gave him a cash allowance for it.

Most tractor collections got their start when the farmer's

granddad pursued the same unenlightened vocation, the space
behind the shed as a result became an antiquary of the agricult.
The once struggling boxelders have grown into venerable old
dinosaurs, their roots interlock with the machinery, the farmer
can't sell the junk because he can't disengage it from the trees.
The first hundred generations of pigweed and thistle have evolved
to lilacs and artichokes, residue of the great artichoke boom some
time back, the fever has passed but the artichokes are doing fine.

Among the collection is a nice patch of big blue stem and
some blue-eyed grass and ox-eye daisies, and the tractors and
other machinery have rusted into the muted color of mahogany
and russet apples. And though the current farmer has spent a couple hundred bucks outfitting a play-yard for his kids, complete
with swings, sandbox, teeter-totter, jungle gym, and playhouse,
they don't use it, instead trundle off to the tractor cemetery and
play for hours among the ancients of agriculture. It has always
been this way.

According to C. H. Wendel's classic volume *Encyclopedia of
American Farm Tractors* there have been in the course of Yankee
agriculture 821 tractor companies— this between the arrival of the
internal combustion engine and the stock market crash of '29. Here
was agriculture's halcyon, when farming occupied center stage,
when the rural village meant farm and middle class meant farmer.

Eight hundred and twenty-one tractor companies. Every self-
respecting village and hamlet in the Midwest had at least an
attempt, it was a totem of modern intellect, a matter of prestige
and a sign of the new agriculture. The American Midwest held the
world's rapt attention for its productivity and innovation, whether
seeds, field practices and of course tractors. The energy of the
farm sector inspired innovation, in turn expanding production and
encouraging an ever new fever of mechanical dementia.

At the center was the tractor, nothing so fired the imagination,
loyalty and hope of the farm community as the tractor. If farmers

in times before sat around the crackerbarrel telling legends of the mightiest urge of muscle God ever fit to horse legs, the next generation of farmers in their crackerbarrel-moods succumbed to tractors. Were they lies? Not entirely. They were myths, these tellings, necessary and justifiable lies. It is sorta easy to get carried away when telling how many acres your tractor plowed in a day, how easy a favorite "Old Rip" was to start, ever so cheap to run, and how never a wrench touches it except to change the oil. Among these tales and outright felonies are remembrances of tractors with lovely names; Moline, Peerless, Rumley, Scientific, names that capture the mood of another time and its ardent hopes.

Ask a farmer what was the highest moment of agricultural science, assuming the notion isn't an oxymoron…ask a farmer what turned agriculture from Cromagnon, hoe-handle, loin-cloth agriculture to modern, bin-busting agriculture and they will not mention hybrid seeds, genetic engineering or barnyard run-off but tractors. Historians, archivists, journalists will suggest other reasons. According to the practitioners it was tractors. Big tractors, little tractors, sighing, dying theatrical tractors, earth-churning, sky-smoking, hot-hitch tractors. Tractors dragged agriculture out of the Ages into the sweet light of enamel paint and down payments. Tractors are what raised rural livelihoods to more pursuits than is customarily honorable among farmers and made it possible for rural people to die of genuine old age and a good share of them as like to get killed off by their newly acquired leisure.

Minnesota for reasons known only to Minniesorts gave birth to the most tractor companies, perhaps for the same reason it inspired the most bachelor farmers. One hundred and nine different tractor companies in Minnesota, Illinois had sixty-three, Ohio eighty-one, Indiana forty-six, Iowa forty-six, Kansas ten, Pennsylvania ten, Maine one. Tractor manufacturing was a Midwest contagion, somewhere northwest of the Ohio and this side of the Platte; maybe it was the soil, the length of day, a tendency toward

abolition, temperance, tinkering, and Calvinism. A high percent-
age of the Midwestern economy did remain agricultural long after
the settlement period, the climate favored crop production and the
transportation of commodities well served by river, rail, roads, and
lake boat. This intrinsic vitality provided the initial pulse for a
tractor company in nearly every city and village. And behind it all
was the hunger for "engines," they didn't much care where they
came from as long as there were plenty.

The tractor company followed in the wake of the village blacksmith, since King Canute the origin of farm implements. Iron
mongering combined with simple wood construction yielded up
the drags, ploughs, clod-busters, hay-forks, and wagons. Black-
smiths followed a natural evolution from forge to hammer works,
slowly expanding their facilities and products; what had been a
horse livery became the source of sprayers, thrashers, hay-rakes,
steel plows, and tractors.

These early tractor companies did not develop their own
engines, instead purchased them from larger manufacturers who
were building engines for a broad range of uses: electrical generation, stationary power, and water pumping. The Charter, Hart-Parr,
Buffalo-Pitts, Kermath, Climax, Red Wing, Beaver, Waukesha-
Hesselman, Continental, and Hercules, to name just a few. Remnants of the Iron Age, slow turning and oil splashing engines with
obscure and not always inducible alchemies for carburetion and
ignition.

The benefits of engine-driven agriculture were immediately
perceivable; milk production increased dramatically with the addi-
tion of high protein corn silage, but only if the farmer used Joseph
Dicks' amazing "Blizzard." Or the Eli Hay Press "with a capacity
of one hundred tons per day" (the user measures the day length at
his own risk) "capable of baling straw as fast as it emerges from
the largest thrasher and yet only one man required to operate it."
Why should any farmer shuck corn by hand when he can have a

Taylor Red Devil corn picker? One man (with the Red Devil) can pick in a morning what ten hell-bent men could not. A long list of tractor-dependent implements quickly supplanted any comparison to horse-drawn agriculture; threshing machines, feed mills, wood saws, mowers, rakes, sprayers, hay presses, silo fillers, choppers, rock pickers, potato diggers, dredges, shovels, cement mixers, irrigation pumps....Farmers knew the millennium had struck. Tractors changed everything. Never mind the rest of the world counted time as B.C. or A.D., for agriculture the ages were either B.T. or A.T., Before Tractor or After. Never mind no one else understood, the farmer did.

It is not surprising that farm implements were named extravagantly, promising wealth, new freedom and maybe ease: Liberty, Commonsense, Cyclone, Pioneer, and the Rose. All the farmer needed to belong to the new enlightenment was a tractor, so the smithy became a tractor company. Required was only a minor extension of the skills found in every blacksmith. The engines were robust and simple, bolt them to a frame, add wheels, drive chain, and a means to steer it. The sorcerer's apprentice had returned and was making tractors. From steel angle, iron plate, and a bucket of bolts came those Cretins, born in a hail of sparks, and almost breathing, a bend, a cut, a notch, a hole, a riveted plate. Every village had its wizard who watched as their black creation crawled out the door under its own power. At the door stood a farmer willing to buy it.

The hundreds of tractors had dozens of different engines, most of which worked and some a good deal better than others. Maybe they did sling oil and smoke and rant, or burn away the driver's clothing and cough enough sparks to threaten a dry landscape. Some started hard, others with unbelievable ease. Seldom did any one builder solve all the technical problems of a traction device whose task was dirt and somehow to survive dirt.

Tractors had a complex set of demands on them, several

seemed at exact cross purposes. A tractor that can admirably pull a plow can not necessarily get to the field with any haste. The early builders struggled with the problems of power transmission, the separate demands for traction, road speed, power take-off, belt pulleys and lift-arms, all from the self-same machine. Rarely did any one tractor accomplish all the needs. If one pulled a plow without compare it wasn't worth spit on the belt.

Among the 821 tractorsmiths in America, a few were pure, uncut snake oil, tractors so awfully pretty in the brochure but when hitched to a plow refused to move. The gears whirred, the chains rattled but the thing sat there immobilized by its own glory. If farmers went broke tractors contributed their share. Did it make a farmer to feel modern if he went bust by way of drought, pestilence, freeze, or flood? For a hundred generations before it had done no different. There is no stature in drought or getting beat-up by the same old-fashioned, God-made forces. It proved nothing of the farmer's modern sensibility, nothing of his technological achievements, his mechanical prowess. Required was a tractor, a Gargantua of pin-striped sheet-metal with red wheels, a nickel-plated exhaust and a seat as high off the ground as a haystack. Now he was modern, set apart from the ages before, mounted on his temple from which to survey agriculture, a darn better reason for going broke.

Their names are worthy sanctification, Lord Almighty did these tractors have names…the Hero, Ploughmaster, the Wolverine, the Wizard, nineteen different manufacturers called their product the American. Every emotion and battle had its namesake. The Alamo and Waterloo, the Beaver, Bear, Bulldog and Bean. Centaur, Champion, and Chief. Eagle, Earthmaster, and Empire. Globe, Giant, Groundhog, Homer Hercules, Hoosier. Peerless, Pocahontas, Samson, Scientific, Uncle Sam, Victory, Yuba, and Zelleo.

What farmer could fail to identify with a tractor named the Toehold, reflecting as it did his own passionate resolve? What farmer doubted what he and ol' Toehold might together make of spring and forty acres of tillable land?

It was all so different from horse agriculture. Man and machine were a fulfillment of human intellect and a good measure of art. Besides being efficient and adaptable tractors were a gentler agriculture, they were cleaner, didn't require the might of God to shoe, and there never was yet a horse born with a PTO shaft.

The tractor proved something to farmers about where they stood, not only in society but in the universe. The substance on which he stood wasn't just earth any longer but a dose of iron plate. Maybe something of a new sense, maybe not, a wonderful sort of greed, a greed to see yourself on such a bright and joyful machine. To pull loose at last from the beasts and gain the seat of the new heaven, the one shaped in iron and stamped Minneapolis Moline.

Once there were eight hundred and twenty-one tractor companies, and once every farmer dreamed of what it would be like to sit on the throne, of a tractor.

Lightning Rods

They were gargoyles, ornamental iron and broken stone as much as flesh and blood. Their eyes rove frantic in their skulls, their faces turned ever upward for signs of a brooding sky. Ozone unbreathable as mud followed after them clinging to their dark hopes and awful predictions. Their victims were barns and granaries and the lonely farmhouses, buildings a bit too prominent because fields made them so, too proud against the vault of sky. And when the farmer surrendered, these grotesques scrambled on the ridgerows, raised their hammers and fought the unjust heaven, taught the sky to mind, and sent the gods home— their sharp knives and sticks taken from them.

They were like rainmakers but they were not rainmakers. Theirs was not to beckon cloud and implore storm but to spend it, to turn it back, send it away, cheat its power. Like rainmakers they came when the signs were right and the congregation was ready. Signs? Surely they knew the signs. A barn had burned last week near Merrill, second one in the county that very week. At Colby lightning touched off a barn and a loafing shed and burned the haystacks out of spite.

The tight billfold pockets of farmers cringed when they heard, their hams crawled, and their chests turned clammy, their nose hairs bristled at the stink of barn burning. Grown men who had seen horrors enough and were not much bothered, had dreams of lightning, of bolts flaring across the sky and of barns afire. They had not slept well the entire week and woke with a start, sweated to their bedclothes.

They knew how well barns burned and rumors of burning fouled the sleep of farmers in the long summers when storms came with vengeful timbre. The sky, they knew, had seen their barns and was waiting for them to have it full. A barn the wind couldn't touch, but lightning could.

What the dark men were called is indistinguishable, nothing as old and rotten with lore as rainmaker or skyshaker. No label was ever quite the measure of their calling. Sometimes it was rodman or ridge runner. I have heard them called sparkies and lightning catchers but the labels have no royal pedigree, they were after all only lightning rod salesmen.

But they were more than salesmen. They were saviors, apostles and missionaries in the land of the unsaved barn. Theirs was not the witching of rainmaker, those antic, imploring gestures appeared the futile attempt. Theirs was a money-back guarantee. No sleepwalking dowser shuffling barefoot in the barnyard. Theirs, by- god, was science, the best electromagnetic protection physics had to offer and guaranteed to protect the barn from lightning or the second set is free.

They came into the farmyards in pickup trucks that had known many gravel roads. A gaunt boy was asleep on the seat, when they shut off the ignition the truck engine let out a grateful sound. It was almost dark when they drove up the farmlane. They knew before they came the clouds were loitering on the horizon. Miscreant as clouds are sometimes. The farmer heard the clouds laughing, snide, cruel laughter, how it hurt his supper. He was thinking of going to bed when the lightning rod salesman arrived, the hand-painted sign on the truck read, Evangeline Lightning Rods, Protects All.

As a salesman his was a slow-motion sell, in a vague and sinister way, as if the very instant the farmer said no the clouds on the horizon would know of his disobedience. The lightning rod salesman acted as if he didn't care in the least whether the farmer bought. Twice he stooped to look at the barn through the windshield, the same dismissing glance survivors use on a corpse. Said the lightning rods came in three different styles to compliment the barn, all of the best free-electron base metal. The farmer recalled a story in the paper, how a fire at Colby had ruined the man entirely. He didn't even ask how much they cost because it hardly seemed to matter.

Sometimes it wasn't so easy and the lightning rod salesman used another approach. Asking in a suggestive way whether the farmer knew there was enough electrical energy in one stroke to power the entire state of New York for a week.

One stroke?

Yes sir. One average eeelectrical storm can supply all the nation's need for eeelectricity.

The salesman noted how the situation isn't any better on account of all the flat land where, the first thing a cloud sees is a barn. His barn. The farmer knew that.

How under these conditions meson particles are unusually prominent, the more so if soil conditions are dry. The farmer knew that too.

Without natural prominences and the asphalt roof shingles the situation is even more accentuated allowing the electron charge in the barn to intensify, almost like a bubble of flammable gas.

Any farmer who did not buy lightning rods under these circumstances was exposing himself and barn to a prolapsed nimbo cumulus, not to mention restless night. All that untamed energy wandering loose out there, collecting its pagan energy to the windward and aimed any dark night at your barn.

The brochure said nickel-plated electrodes never rust and have no equal in the conductor field except gold plate, the farmer liked the sound of that. If he was gonna set up an altar on the ridgerow of his barn it might as well be nickel-plate.

The salesman droned on…how a patented system actually forces lightning back into the cloud, deflects the perturbation in the eye of the storm, it will not strike your barn but shore-as-heck the next barn downwind is in greater peril.

So that was it? A barn without lightning rods is catching the damnation of barns with lightning rods! Didn't seem fair somehow, teasing a cloud, then turning the thing loose on a neighbor. If one barn had a lightning rod, they all had to out of self-preservation.

Together they walked over to the pickup truck; the farmer had to choose. The Emperor style lightning rods stood five foot high with nickeled spires and jeweled glass balls. The end of the rod was tipped with black enamel broad-arrows. The set of five came with a free weathervane, the pointer of filigree iron in the same black enamel.

The second set was plainer, no broad-arrows, no crystal globes, no windvane, and stood only two feet high. The third model was little more than a series of white metal spikes, hardly worth considering. The premium model cost twenty-two fifty, ten dollars more than the basic set, which the salesman did say would probably work as well…

Probably is an awful narrow gap when the spark plug is a sky with its back up, most of it headed this way. It is better than even odds the farmer wouldn't have a plain set on his barn. The knight-errant of the Evangeline Lightning Rod Company knew that. Fact is, he had never sold a basic economy model.

One hundred and twelve dollars fifty cents for a complete set including grounding wire. Normal spacing is one rod every twenty linear feet, with 10 percent discount for cash payment the day the work is done. Everyone knew cash meant cash, not check, not credit card, not installment but a wad of damp bills in the man's pocket. The farmer already knew the total, had done it in his head.

The next morning the crew came in another stale pickup truck. They unloaded the extension ladder and by the time it was tipped against the barn the grounding rod was already eight feet in. A ridge devil nailed home the rod braces while another threw down the grounding cable. Twenty minutes later it was done, the pale violet glass catching the light and the weather arrow already squeaking.

It'll work in after awhile and you won't hear it anymore, meaning the squeak.

The farmer parted with one hundred one, fifty cash, they shook hands and the gargoyles were gone.

Fifty years since and the barn still hasn't been struck by lightning. Neither has the neighbor's barn, which doesn't have lightning rods, which proves…the neighbor is lucky? Lightning rods are fraudulent? Or that clouds aren't trying very hard? Who knows?

The nickel-plated electrodes along the barn's spine became the place after awhile. A look of defiance is about them watchful as sentries on a guard tower. One hundred one, fifty is money well-spent even if it is only ridgerow art. The wind arrow is good to look to first thing every morning and it still squeaks but the farmer knows when the wind has turned its mind.

A Waning Soul

L ord Harold died last week. It was about time, I guess, though I did hope he'd hang on awhile longer but at the same time I realize this is how it works.

Lord Harold died routine enough back in 1968, his wake held at the Boston Parlor in the back of the furniture store whose close association provided mourners with some of the most accommodating sorrow. Boston's being where the Protestant side of the township conducted their grief and dismissal, been this way for most of a century.

A heart attack killed Lord Harold. He was driving home in a pickup from Plainfield, the truck veered off the road and went swimming in the Buena Vista. Was a Ford. None of this woulda happened if he'd been driving a Chevy.

Lord Harold lived on the Maine Road, last place before the road goes to gravel. Was Lord Harold who owned Old Slab, only dog ever to vote at the annual town meeting, his wife being Myrtle and her kitchen the one the town crew found its way to every winter morning plump in their mackinaws. Harold's was the last contact with the civil world before striking across the uncertainty of the Buena Vista Marsh. In the time before citizens band and cellular, the muck ran a whole heck farther across than it does now, Myrtle's kitchen the last chance to get warm and coincidentally load up on her famous lard doughnuts fresh that very morning and laying in a cake pan lined with a flour sack atop a woodstove the size of the HMS "Resolute," this cast-iron dreadnought fired by corn cobs.

Farmers I believe understand death from a different vantage as do villagers. According to urban sensibilities Lord Harold was dab dead once the box is shoveled over, the sandy loam on the coffin lid sufficient to keep him that way, never mind the exchange of blood for embalming fluid. This ain't how the agricult sees the event. Sure enough Lord Harold is legally dead and his pipe smoking days over, but a thick residue of the man clings to the farmship as can't be scraped off by death alone. Meaning he wasn't entirely toast. Sometimes a farmer is harder to kill off than a pasture gone to quack.

Take Willie who died, oh musta been in the '60s some time, his place eighty rods up from Lord Harold's. Willie planted a couple rows of white pine around his farm in the late '50s. Soon became a fossil himself, the house burnt and the remains bulldozed level with the field. The reason Willie isn't full length dead is that hedgerow of white pine has grown to darn handsome timber. Ain't a morning in summer I don't greet him and he wave back. A red-tail took up a nest in the burr tree on the east forty. Not a day gone to hell and irrigating that row of white pine hasn't tried to soften to a contentment taters alone can't offer.

What I'm saying is there ain't no lingering like what a dead farmer can provoke. Take my grandfather's first barn. It be no more than a shack and the exact as when he lived, a perverse building out behind the brooder coop and standing there going on a hundred and fifty years. Been used as a barn, smithy, woodshed, ice house, and fertilizer storage. When we started with bag fertilizer that shack held the entire spring's measure; now it wouldn't hold enough to last till noon.

The building has plagued the farm going on four generations 'cause someone made the mistake of a seamless galvanized roof. Ain't a farmer in hell or Topeka who is without sense to know a good roof is a sin to waste. It's an unwritten commandment not to pillage anything with a decent roof since you never know when a good roof might be just the wrench you're looking for.

This is why an ugly, god-forsaken shed has been hanging around the farm long after common sense suggests otherwise. We've tried every fool trick to ease it to demise but the darn thing won't go. It wasn't ever painted but once in a fit of unconscious tidiness I painted the shed. Those boards sucked up red latex like it was chocolate malt and weren't satisfied till ten gallons had elapsed, this on a shed a long-handled lawn mower won't fit to.

After I painted it you could almost hear my ancestors groan. Not only has the shack seamless galvanized that ain't shown a sign of decay since Second Corinthians, but now had a quarter inch layer of the finest red latex; we're talking wholesale immortality here.

The reason Lord Harold didn't die straight away was he kept pigeons. This isn't exactly true being as no farmer honestly keeps pigeons. Pigeons aren't a voluntary act. Somehow pigeons arrived at his barn and silo and in that first generation imprinted to their genes the instinct of Lord Harold's place on the nether end of the Maine Road and cherished for generations like pigeons are prone to. The neat trick about instinct is it reduces the brain size necessary to life without crippling the animal with too much intelligence.

Every farmer comes to a decision about pigeons: either they are this side of twenty-two caliber or the other side. Some do not love pigeons as much as they doubt the wisdom of twenty-two caliber in the vicinity of their barn. Pigeons often as not win by default. This leads in turn to resignation and the pigeons as a result have a homeland. Once a pigeon has taken root to the horizon of that barn or silo there ain't no process, chemical or psychological, as can uproot it. Transported to the ends of the earth, a

pigeon will find its way home or die trying; the pigeon is I believe
a semi-Jewish animal.

Lord Harold's barn had the prettiest ventilator of any barn
around, stood a story and a half tall on its own right, not including
the nose cone and filigree windvane with gothic letters.

Like pigeons everywhere, Harold's flock suffered cats, owls,
disease, power lines, road salt, hawks, peregrines, frustrated duck
hunters, moldy corn, and no corn. The populace swelled, then
dimmed at a hard winter only to blossom riotously again. At
length a kind of stability reigned, this what some proclaim as the
mysterious balance of ecology. It wasn't ecology as much as cats
and their enhancement or frustration as compounded by distemper.
Some cats were destined to the hunt and some were not. Some
stalked pigeons, others thought pigeons were an unworthy game
and too blame high anyway. And even a cat can be born vegetarian
and possess a higher moral conscience right along with Henry
David Thoreau without any of the literary bother.

When Lord Harold died the flock continued as if they hadn't
noticed his obituary in the newspaper. Myrtle rented out the place
and went to work as a cleaning lady, an otherwise odious fate
except farmwives generally find the change is positive, a benefit
to free time and spending money…which doesn't say a lot for
agriculture.

Those pigeons ranged and flew and circled and hooved and
dove and swooped and tumbled and all the other g-force antics of
pigeons, living high and mighty in Lord Harold's barn. Harold
may have been most dead but not entirely. Every morning those
pigeons rose with first light to circumnavigate the farmship and
descend like the breath of creation itself to every new plowing.

Eventually a high velocity tater man bought Lord Harold's
farm and in a fit of expediency gutted out the farmstead. Cleared
the woods as had been there since the Pleistocene and for the first
time in recorded history the smoke of the paper mills of yonder

river town was stood visible all the way to the moraine. There is no worse scene on earth than impending municipality.

The house went through a series of renters, my favorites were the cash-cropping hippies who raised herbs in the barnyard and made tater prospecting look dim-witted by comparison. Weren't Columbian Gold but it was dizzy enough. Every year they threw an enormous party complete with some rabid boys on Harleys who adorned their arms with museum quality etchings. Their womenfolk were interesting too.

Lord Harold died out entirely when a renter with genocide in his heart took a sixteen gauge to the pigeons.

Some hold the soul is immortal; it isn't. The purpose of soul ain't immortality as much as companionable linger. Souls haunt a place for awhile and when it doesn't fit any more, it leaves. The soul is like a warped boomerang—sometimes when you throw it, it won't come back.

Still, I wasn't ready for Lord Harold being all the way dead. I liked the morning better for the pigeons of his barn lifting what was left of the dark and hauling it away to burn in the dawn. The sky and earth are emptier now. I know the hawk in the burr tree mourns Lord Harold's last passing as much as a hawk can mourn anything.

Soul I understand, but immortality with a seamless galvanized roof is another heck. If you want to curse future generations with more worn out sheds than they'll know what to do with, dress it up in seamless galvanized.

Origin of the Potato Digger

Every October up at St. Adelbert's in Rosholt they hold the Mass of St. Arthur, who performed a most companionable miracle in so much as farmers are concerned. This isn't the Arthur of dragons who oughta be ashamed for extinguishing such a remarkable beast, rather St. Arthur of Antigo who kilt off the rear-end draggin' dragon. Killed off the October monster who comes out of his lair when summer is down to the short string and there's a heck peck potatoes to save.

Potatoes are a specialized curse and people who follow the vegetable know this. Every other vegetation, having human welfare in mind, has the decency to grow above ground, where a farmer with too much on his mind for intrigues only has to grab at it. Like wheat and tomatoes and Harelson apples, like cabbage, sweet corn and snap beans.

Taters tend to burrow. Because they're half Irish and predisposed to felonious behavior: sneaking, conniving, and avoiding daylight. The potato is closer related to the angleworm and the gopher than to Durham wheat or hubbard squash.

Any agricultural entrepreneur can tell you, industry does not and can not commence with a six-tine fork. For generations the potato was a clandestine activity while wheat ruled a million acres and yellow corn a million more, followed by okra, spinach, and rhubarb. All of America be eatin' grits and the french fry left undiscovered had the tater maintained its six-tine fork attitude.

Was a farmer near Straybuck, Maine, who believed he had found the remedy. In the spring when he planted the taters, he buried chicken bones among the rows. Idea being to turn a pack of keen-nose terriers on the field at the optimum moment. Didn't work out this way, seems potatoes and chicken bones ripen at different velocities.

Walter C. Galenburg of Antigo attempted the next major improvement, he installed in his tater patch an even distribution of kinetic materials. The more casual term is dynamite. When the crop appeared ready, Walter sat on the plunger. As you might guess, he did not so much invent the potato digger as the potato masher.

Walter's brother Arthur lived across the road and was a sight more contemplative than his elder sibling. Arthur knew from the outset dynamite wasn't the answer though it did alleviate quackgrass with more splash than routine cultivation.

Arthur, being a thoughtful length of farmer, spent a good deal of his waking hours in his repair shop, which some attribute to his selection of semi-naked calendars. So much time in fact that Arthur's devotion had the appearance of a monastic order, 'ceptin' wrenches and drill bits at first Mass. All this being possible because his shop stove kept Antigo winters at bay. Arthur spent every off-season thinking how in tarnation an honest man might rouse taters from the ground without resorting to fork, dogs, or dynamite.

The story is Arthur got the idea from a hay elevator, making the empirical leap to a continuous chain with its snout in the ground and its tail wagging—kinda like a dog digging out a badger hole but with grease cups added.

The next fall Arthur had his experimental model and the horses educated to pull it, and darn if the thing didn't work. For most of thirty rods before the chain packed up. Chain was the answer but not hay chain, not manure spreader chain, another kind of rough service chain was needed.

For years Arthur labored, trying all manner of designs; chain with links, chain with rings, he tried everything but shoelaces. Arthur took to sleeping in the shop, consumed by the quest of a reliable potato digger. Hardly ever did he come to the house except for supper and then so backfired and hammered the hair on his arms smelled like singed feathers. Arthur's wife coulda run a bordello off the front porch and Arthur wouldna noticed.

The problem, as every farmer knows, is not so much to get a contraption to dig potatoes but continue doing so. No other crop is so cursed. Were the tubers grown among revolving whet-stones the erosion to the implement would be no greater. Digging potatoes ground up equipment, rendering it dust long before its time.

Story goes, Arthur came in the house late on the Saturday night Miss Baginski was getting legally hitched and, what with the dance and the barrel, it looked to be the social event of the season. Arthur wasn't only late but stinking of sheet metal. This where Mother Galenberg took the stove poker to him, narrowly missing his person with a swipe, winding the end over the handle of the cistern pump. Arthur glances at the curled end and a thousand watts of eureka shine on his face. He grabs the poker and rushes pell-mell from the house. Missus Galenberg all this while mortified on seeing how narrowly she missed the punch line to Arthur's obituary.

Tater farmers everywhere know what Arthur beheld is the double helix erotic garter snake hook of the industrial grade potato digger. A curve so complex few farmers can duplicate it with a paper clip without sneaking a look at the original. No mere fish hook, instead a Chinese puzzle of a hook. A slink so curvaceous as takes a whisky-bathed salamander to duplicate. Granted, it still suffered erosion pretty bad and woe to the farmer who didn't mind the slack in his chain, soon after the entire length gathered in a bundle tighter than buttons on a bartender's vest.

In the northern regions, where the potato is the last resort of agriculture, there are services in October to saints not listed in the Vatican directory. Where the dismissal of the six-tine is right up there with full-frontal resurrection when it comes to a nice short-cut. As any can see, a specialized point of reference; a world view only forty acres of hand-digging can inflict.

On Finding God

Harry P. owned the prettiest barn in the universe. Not merely the prettiest in North America or in the solar system but the prettiest in the whole dad-gum universe. Harry lived east of the Liberty Corners kirk in Valley Up where he was indentured to the third pew from the front. Harry being lay leader sat nearest the pulpit of any member of the congregation, a tad hard of hearing Harry was but not so much to sit in the front pew.

Sitting in the front pew according to the unwritten rules of this kirk bordered on sacrilege. God didn't want people sitting too blame close to the altar owing it showed a lack of mortification. If a person isn't a little afraid then they ain't humble and if you ain't a little afraid you don't need God. After all, God is for the handicapped, the wounded, and the vulnerable, which is why the kirk had more than its fair share of farmers on the membership roll. Because farmers feel so blame vulnerable.

Harry's barn started out as Harry's dad's barn, which is how most barns start. A plain barn at the outset, it prospered and went on to set suckers like a boxelder so by the time I knew Harry's barn it covered an estimated four acres. It wasn't a single barn at all but a lummox of barns, hanging off in every cardinal direction, all of it high roofed and red.

Harry P. was baptized in two religions, one of them being hymn-prone methodee, his other was barn paint. The joy of Harry's life expressed itself in Chinese Red. How many gallons he consummated in his lifetime is unknown, an astronomical number, surely a geological one. His junk pile back in the corner of the alfalfa field overflowed with paint cans. When one of the neighbors required a can for fence staples or bent nails, they snuck off to Harry's pile and secured a half dozen. Harry never stopped painting his barn. On the sand side of the Moore Hill they said cruel things about Harry's barn. How being so dash over-big it put off the dawn half an hour for those west of the barn's flank. Weren't true. Morning came the same. Wasn't Harry's barn doing shadow but the moraine. But you can't blame a moraine as you can insult a barn a whole heck bigger than any barn ought to be, especially one so regularly painted.

Another thing they said about Harry's barn was you could always find fresh paint on it. From May to September Harry's idle moments got spent painting. Most days it was China Red, on others Episcopalian White for the trim and hex boards. As a result there wasn't anything more vibrant this side of a circus tent or train wreck than Harry's barn. It glowed. The barn was the first thing you'd see coming over Moore Hill. There, east of the kirk the critical fusion of that barn. Harry's barn brighter than Blake's tiger burning bright in the forest of the night.

How it caught fire nobody knows. Harry had died some years previous and his barn started down the awful fate waiting on all barns. The paint had finally dried and when you drove by, there were cats in the windows looking quizzical. Might have been the cats who tipped over a jar and the shard caught the sun the same as a magnifying glass. More likely it was the wiring where a rat chewed through. Still it is a mystery for if there were cats there wonna been rats neither.

It caught fire, Harry's barn did. Early evening. September. I remember seeing the glow on the horizon; a sunrise at eventide that voluminous was a fire. The trees on the moraine cast shadows and the sunflowers in the garden turned as if anticipating a new day.

Harry's was the biggest barn fire in the history of the township. Everybody was there. For two miles either way the road choked with cars parked cross-strawed. The fire department madder than hell 'cause they couldn't get the big pumper in, not that it mattered 'cause everybody knows you can't save a barn. Seemed almost a sacrilege to try.

Every vowel the earth ever uttered was said that night by Harry's barn. Dinosaur sounds, Indian war whoops, whale song. The barn pleaded, it whimpered, it raged. It cussed, it swore and paused for more. Every language, every dialect tried, there was no saving it. Was then I heard Harry's barn pray. All great things do, you know. I saw it bow and close its eyes, then give its soul to the skies.

I was not the only one who wept while watching Harry's barn burn. The fire spied the tears on the thousand faces turned. Was in all this I saw God come and sit, and watch the spectacle as only God can. He crossed his knees and leaned back, pondering the way gods do. When he rose and turned to go I do not know, the barn was more interesting and slow.

The winter passed before the fire went out. Barn fires are that way. When smolder gets in hay.

The World's Biggest Birdhouse

Great Da built it, that being in 1901, outta timber from the swamp woods and the loving touch of Freddie Taylor, barn builder. This when Great Da was a sleekit man full of hope and boiled cabbage.

Maybe it was '02 he built the barn, can't rightly say 'cause barns ain't the sort of monstrosity as gets born sudden. Barns happen the same way as Genesis, which the Book don't know nothing about. About the dark side of creation meaning the swamp and saw timber back there as never knew fitful breeze being so awful deep in the primeval shade, the sort of timber a fearful man wants to rouse a barn of.

Great Da didn't call it a barn, his word was byre as means the same thing as barn 'cepting barn's a Saxon word, which Scotsblood don't like to utter more than once a year in the case it is infectious.

Forty-eight wide and one hundred and forty long, this the classic measure every Christian knows, the very same for Noah's barn give or take a cubit. This volume being necessary if prosperity is to be accomplished using God's line and measure. A barn that'd hold course in any wind, against any damnation, proud and painted up as any red-lipped braw. A proud thing is a barn, the sort a ploughman can hitch to the horizon. A barn as can seduce rain out of drought-ridden summer or with its shaming eye turn away an ill-tempered cloud, minding the storm to go by way of Arnott or some other detour but not over this man's byre.

Great Grand Da, long syne pushing up grass and sandburrs beheck the village, never intended the barn for a birdhouse. A barn is liable to attract riffraff and loafers same as loose change attracts lawyers. Couldn't hardly blame pigeons for taking up with a barn being as it pretty much blocked their passage, protruding as it did halfway to the moon and about as wide across as Mt. Everest.

This how come Great Da did sell every chicken the farmstead put up, sold at village prices all neeked and shucked and not save a single lizard 'cause this paranormal barn did suck in doves by the multitude from six townships over. Doves as feast on the neighbor's rye and thatch with a lot less inputs than a cow or chicken. There was squab enough for home and relation and not a shilling did he spend, the barn done it all 'cause he followed God's measure.

The situation only got worse when Great Da built the silo—oh how pigeons do love a silo. The beastie won't nest in a tree like any honest length of feather, tree ain't high enough for 'em. What they want is the peak of the barn or better yet, the silo a full ten leagues above the prairie. Don't matter if farmkids potted them with twenty-twos or cats gobbled down the fledglings, there was always more pigeons, happy and content as pigeons can be.

What made the barn a birdhouse wasn't the pigeons, neither was it the sparrows as nestled in the eaves, nor the starlings as took up housekeeping in the armpit of every joist and rafter. What made the barn the biggest birdhouse in the history of Audubon were swallows. If Great Da's barn had legions of pigeons, plagues of sparrows, volleys of starlings, miscellaneous owls, wrens, woodpeckers, it had veritable rain of swallows. Every eave had its tenement row, every beam in the cow alley was festooned with adobe dwellings. Not neat single-file rows of civilized swallows but claim-jumping, subletting, squatter-type swallows, borough and borough, ghetto after ghetto, suburb on suburb of swallows. There ain't no creature of earth as enjoys slum conditions better than swallows.

A person could have pulled every nail and hickory pin from that barn and it'd stand nevertheless, cemented together by countless swallow nests. Glued in place by bird spit.

A summer barn is not a happy place. In its confines are sweating cows, a swarm cloud of flies, liberal amounts of animal mud whose resulting humidity would insult the rainforest. A closer rendition of damnation you can not find on earth this side of a Bessemer converter. The only element mollifying this scene of woebegone were the swallows hovering at every niche. Zooming and slashing through the air in a banquet of aerobatics. Their flight resembled the oriental calligraphy without the mess of ink. Swallows don't just fly, they waltzed and pirouetted. Tango and waltz and mamba. Milking cows in this hell more humid than the bearded lady's armpit wasn't any the cooler but it was entertaining.

There were in the neighborhood farmers who took hop poles to the swallow nests and smashed them down. God musta hated folks like that 'cause their barns caught fire more often than the barns of farmers who let swallows be. 'Course everybody knows you can't burn mud anyway.

Great Grand Da's barn is going on a hundred years old and in its tenure seen a million swallows, ten million sparrows, three point seven million starlings and thirty-five million pigeons, not counting the squab as went for supper. A hundred years that barn has prospered birds with every nook, cranny and mud puddle. On its own architecture I believe it should have fallen down a half century ago, instead preserved, rendered buoyant against every hostile cloud and saber-toothed blizzard. A hundred years and still standing, one hundred and forty by forty-eight, the biggest gosh darn birdhouse in the world.

Exquisite Barbarian

According to an old rural proverb, some things deserve sanctification more than the martyrs who preached in heathen lands. On this list of other saints is garden rhubarb; *rha barbarum,* literally barbarian rheum, rheum the description of any plant with a watery or juice sap.

Rhubarb from its introduction to the West in the 1400s was a poltice, "...the phisicious with a lyttell Rhubarbe purge many humours of the body" (1540). "...take Rasne (raisins) and Rhubarbe and grynde it togedre..." (1533). By the time of settlement of the New World, rhubarb was a well established member in the herb garden..."that every household in the north ought for health...have..."

Rhubarb found its way into pamphlets with titles like "Prosperous Homesteading," which for a dime guaranteed the prospective emigrant success in the west lands. Those unable to read bought them as a good omen for the trek, never mind the authors had never been farther west than the Eddystone Light.

To plant the homestead with the well known root seemed sound advice. This generous herb was known to bring cure when no else could. A tonic, a purgative, and a binder, no garden could avail without the barbarian. Rhubarb was an enlightened witchcraft and it naturalized easily in what many settlers came bitterly to realize was an under-reported climate. The plant grew without penitence in Minnesota, it flourished in Kansas, survived an Iowa winter with no more than a shell of horse manure, neither could weeds and prairie grass confound it.

If rhubarb seemed well liked in the European garden during the three hundred years previous, in the New Earth it was adored. The sod house might cherish the lilac, take pride in the apple but what kept them faithful to the bleak horizon was rhubarb, for one superior thing could rhubarb do and do so well and earnestly as to bring accusation of the nether arts.

Rhubarb came in the spring before dandelion and coltsfoot, hardly had watercress greened when rhubarb began to unfurl its grimaced leaves. Never mind the snowbank yet abroad and nights cool enough to freeze a lost calf to death, out ventured this elephant-eared fruit.

How long before rhubarb had been known in the European hamlet is uncertain. What the manor house and Victorians proudly called rhubarbarin, in the American farmlands was less elegantly addressed as pie-plant. At the supper table the dusty ploughman sank his heavy feet and drank the homey brew, its contents nothing more than a lift of water and the free juice of rhubarb. A temperance drink though it was, it swelled the brain and woke the spirit. Those with less resistance made rhubeer, a tangy rheu-flavored infusion to sweep away the weariness of a field-spent day.

Rhubarb had its constituents who invited it to every accident. Drizzled on an open wound the juice was believed to prevent sour infection, applied to a cut it stanched blood flow, never mind the resulting sting might arrest the heart. Rhubarb relieved gout, bladder infection, purged the gut, abetted the owly stomach, shook blackbirds from the brain, and the wine of it inclined the platonic to get on with it. A garden without rhubarb was an unwashed, unsaved heathen indeed.

Whether any knew the secret of rhubarb—vitamin C—they acted as if they did. In farm garden, in village patch, long before the apple tree bloomed much less bore fruit, before mushrooms, peas, lettuce, and suskatoon berries was rhubarb.

Some households favored rhubarb jam, others that plough-man's tonic cut with honey, a choice of jellies or simple puddings. Others chewed the raw stalk itself dipped in sugar, the aesthetic ate it plain. The most favored application was pie. As pie rhubarb is a ghastly object. The vittle resembles the contents of a herbi-vore's stomach little congealed under a crust, as an ill-tempered and toxic concoction. Served plain rhubarb pie put a grown man's body out of joint. Sour isn't word enough for rhubarb. A perme-ation first sensed in the pit of the stomach, transferring to the spinal column where it twists the vertebrae at exact right angles and then is unleashed.

Let sweet cream or whipped address rhubarb pie and the result is just as awful-looking but fabulous to swallow. So it was at the spring supper the extremes of earth meet and like the touch of mat-ter and anti-matter blew the dusty farmer's mind to nothingness. Weariness is forgotten, the furrows yet to plow of no consequence. Eyes close in reverie, the jaw spasms at an unalloyed molecule, and sure it is the rhubarb ministry just saved another soul.

Orange in the Way of Legends—Part I

The Allis Chalmers Tractor Company of West Allis, Wisconsin, was the source of the now mandated color for deer-hunter apparel. The objective was visibility without consideration for social propriety or artistic comportment. The designers knew from the outset the color of their tractor was several hundred thousand degrees above mere visibility: Allis Chalmers driven in the shed, the door pulled close with a stick in the hasp, was visible right through the boards and only a little out of focus. In the time before nuclear power plants and microwaves, an Allis Chalmers was the epitome of indiscriminate radiation, preceding the chartreuse mohawks and wet t-shirt contests of the present age.

If Allis of Allis chose a vicious orange for their product line other tractor companies did the same. The brilliance of the paint job was well known as the deciding factor of the sale. Those tractors glinted like diadems; Minneapolis Molines the color of buttermilk pancakes, John Deeres in the green of the shamrock, the red McCormick Deerings, the jade hypnotic spell of Olivers, and indigo Fords. If horse agriculture could have fought back with hue and cry equal to an orange Allis the tractor might have failed as miserably as the dirigible.

My father committed the salvation of himself and his ilk to the tractor in 1943, a four cylinder, magneto ignition, 4 BTDC, updraft carburetor, four speed non-synchronized Allis Chalmers Model C painted a predatory orange.

As a man of conscience my father spent the six years previous rumbling in his sleep, tortured with thoughts of tractors. For fifty thousand years previous our kind had been dirt farmers, aided throughout by horses: Clydes, Percherons, Morgans, Belgians. It makes little difference if an archaeologist takes the stand and testifies there ain't been farmers for fifty thousand years or dreadnought horses neither; to farmers it felt like fifty thousand years of horses. What roiled my father's sleep was whether or not the historical inertia of farmers including all luck might go bust if switched to tractors. It did not help matters that Uncle Jim spoke eloquently for the Anti-Tractor Party.

Uncle Jim is the only person I ever knew whose body consisted of 99 percent sinew. He possessed no skeleton, neither leg bones nor knee caps, just sinew from gill to dorsal. Uncle Jim was so limber he could pick taters from morning frost till sunset without the least indication of backache, which didn't make complaining sound the least bit credible.

Uncle Jim had issued a curse on tractors, whole township knew it. The curse weren't said outright or published in the Daily, it was a curse all the same. The gist being any farmer attempting tractors from the Republican section of the township was gonna die, his barn burn, his outhouse fill up, his kitchen chimney fall through the floor, his cows go dry and his tater bin rot all in direct proportion to the farmer's treason, his denial of horses and new allegiance to tractors.

According to Uncle Jim, Mother Nature was not in the mood to suffer tractors. If a heifer won't take, if the oats didn't germinate and blueberries failed to bloom, the reason was tractors. What farmers were trifling with was the ordained order of the universe

plain and simple. If you wanna blast the whole shebang to England then go ahead and harness a tractor.

This bothered my father. For six years he endured recurrent
tractor nightmares and vivid scenes of horsedrawn apocalypse, the
world, holy matrimony and hybrid corn all falling into the pits of
hell on the chance purchase of a tractor.

It might have been easier if Uncle Jim had been less sinewy,
less the fossil look of endurance, less the all-knowing countenance
on him. Uncle Jim owning the thinnest most pathetic stretch of
translucent hide ever pulled over a person, he had a gaze a heck
more than woeful. When he looked at you it seemed the very Rock
of Ages turned in concert with him. The muscles on his eyes
moved with the stealth of the Old Testament, the tendons in his
neck worked like shackle ropes of a thousand crucifixions and
lynchings. He was Mister Judgement, turning to toast with baleful
eyes any who mentioned a tractor in friendly context.

This tortured my father; Uncle Jim might be right. Tractors
could well be the ruin of farmering. With a tractor, Uncle Jim said,
any jack-ass can farm. Rubber tires are gonna ruin America, said
the King of Sinew. Ruin what the God of Scotland and John Knox
had ordained. How can a man sweat sitting on a tractor seat? Wigh,
it's creation outta whack and if you think God is gonna stand for it
without a poke in the eye you got another jostle coming.

All the while Pa dreaming of a brightly robed Minneapolis
Moline, John Deere, McCormick Deering, Ferguson, Oliver,
Massey Harris, and Case of Racine. He chose Allis of Allis for
color alone. He figured as long as he was doing damage to the
universe he might as well do it with the grandest ornament he
could find, meaning the X-ray orange. Then again, it might have
been because Barney Oldfield had driven a Model C Allis
Chalmers around a race track at 64.38 mph. How exactly this per-
tained to plowing loam I did not know and suspect my father
didn't either. Still there is comfort in knowing a tractor can do

hurry when called on, especially if the Four Horsemen are at a gal-
lop from the backside.

All tractors previous to the Allis Chalmers Model C had steel
wheels, which is why they were called tractors in the first place.
Cast iron wheels measuring six foot in diameter with tempered
steel lugs linked via gears to a slow-running engine is the epitome
of Traction. Traction with a capital T. There ain't no end to the pull
of a steel-lugged tractor screwed down into first gear. It was
frightening to think of tractors clawing at the hide of the earth
without respite or leisure. There was even a plan formulated in
Iowa to set fields at right angles to each other so tractors didn't
twist the planet out of shape one spring morning when all that
steel-lugged traction came at once.

The townmen of the farm precincts did not mind tractors but
were not much pleased with the steel wheels. Steel disturbed the
first class grading job on townroads, not to mention what they did
to a fancy asphalt road. The John Deere Company is credited with
the first remedy, removable lugs, in belief a plain steel wheel can't
wreck the road. They demonstrated how in a mere twenty minutes a
man in the field with the proper wrench can fit all thirty lugs to the
driving wheels. Unfortunately those twenty minutes as it turned out
was the bone of contention. Twenty minutes right out of the ripest,
sweetest segment of the morning. Twenty minutes and all the Uncle
Jims in the world rolling horse-drawn furrows so smooth it hardly
mattered the tractor caught up by mid-morning. Those first laps
counted for more than all the rest when it was your neighbor's field
first to turn into damp, sweet aromas. His the field calling out to
loam remembrance buried in the musk of thousand year farmers.

A man with lugs to fit took a beating on such a morning. It
was about here Barney Oldfield took a Model C around a dirt
track at 64.38 mph. Wasn't 64 mph that mattered, what mattered
was 64.38 mph on a tractor. Try that on your John Deere GP, or
McCormick Deering with steel wheels; 64.38 mph on steel with or

without lugs did not exist. With nothing to absorb road shock, a steel-wheeled tractor is no more pleasant to ride than a heifer in heat. Barney Oldfield proved less about velocity than he proved a cure for the spring-plowing lugwrench-blues.

If it hadn't been for the Allis Chalmers Model C on rubber tires half of farming would yet belong to Belgians and Clydes on the merit of the first furrow. With rubber a tractor farmer gained not only the first lap but ten acres plowed by nightfall. He was home early for chores and the field planted by Saturday afternoon if the weather held. And so it happened more horse farmers were killed off by Barney Oldfield than history will ever know.

Orange in the Way of Legends—Part II

U ncle Jim's curse is still in effect. First furrow, important as it is, is not everything. Other questions about a tractor's reliability, simple dilemmas like how do you make a tractor stop? As history amply notes farmers are slow to change. For a million years farmers have been accustomed to shouting *whoa*. A million years of conditioning is hard to displace, children of farmers who never once drove a god-proud plow horse will yet holler *whoa* before hunting out the clutch and binders.

Stopping a tractor was not the only problem farmers had exiting a thousand millennia reign of horsedrawn. Winter starting was another, besides which a horse didn't need a crank. Maybe a few oats and a supply of hay but come morning a horse started, winter or not, unless it was dead and farmers can generally tell the difference. Tractors on the other hand required a full-scale romance to get loose on a winter morning. Actually it took more than romance to get a tractor going at twenty below; foreplay was required. As any can see tractors required the same dismissal of politeness as Salome, who needed the head of John the Baptist to start dancing.

So there were farmers who thought owning a tractor was a public admission of impropriety, which didn't help the early adjournment of the Horse Party. My father's cousin over on the school road used kindling wood. Every winter morning he lit a fire underneath the Case Model 7, kept a spare set of ignition wires hanging in the granary owing that sometimes he over-warmed it. My father used a kerosene lamp set on a block of wood with the chimney kissed against the engine case, the whole thing covered over with a wool quilt. According to plan an hour later the tractor should start after a couple turns. Siegfrid Tecomseh Simonds lost his barn to tractor starting using the kerosene lamp method, same with Alecs MacCrinnons at Lanark and Casimir Cycosh at Polonia. Point in fact more barns, coops, granaries and other sheds lost their lives to tractor starting than to snow load. For quite awhile Uncle Jim ran neck and neck in the great horse/tractor debate.

The main fault of pioneer tractors was their inbred unwillingness to start in the first place. Horses are born idling, a tractor ain't, same as the mule. A tractor must be talked to, cajoled, inspired, feinted, tricked, and any of a dozen other sordid diplomacies. Lots of farmers believed tractors shoulda been designed to run all the time. Maybe turn the engine down to one cylinder and let it run that way and when you want more power, light up the others. Sometimes engineering isn't even close to satisfactory.

The crooked stick protruding from the muzzle of a tractor was not an easy way to start it. Those who designed tractors never turned one over at minus 29 degrees Fahrenheit hoping on the favorable conjunction of mixture and spark. Hand cranking a tractor wasn't so much dangerous as it was suicidal. Lord Harold lost at least one thumb to the reluctance of the Case Model 7. Sooner or later no matter what, that engine cussed out the person on the other end of the handle. Harrison Newby lost his front teeth. Guy Gilson nearly lost his…his…ah…well anyway he sang a high tenor in the church choir long after Nature intended him to settle in another octave.

Starting a tractor gave rise to more inventions bent on circumnavigating the crank than any other act of farming. Howard Oliphant had a quarter ton of red bricks winched 12 foot off his shed floor. He connected this to a relay of cables, thence on to a shaft, on again to a flywheel the exact diameter of the crank handle. At night he drove the tractor into the shed and mated the crank to the hole of his brick-driven automatic-start. The problem with his solution was either the tractor must start the first chance or Howie had to go for Uncle Jim and have his horse drag the tractor off the starting rig. Seems he hadn't figured out a device to raise the bricks with the tractor connected. The other problem was the bricks, that shed weren't intended to levitate a ton of bricks.

Stopping a tractor engine was almost as nerve-wracking as starting it. Most of the early models came with Fairbanks and Morse magnetos, excellent magnetos. Forty-thousand volts of output was commonplace, the same supplied to the telephone company and at a single turn connected Polonia to Amherst despite ten miles of intervening hills. Fairbanks and Morse were good blue-spark magnetos. The theory of halting an engine was to shunt a lever on the back side of the magneto grounding the ignition. Why they did not place the lever on the front side of the magneto should have gained a hearing before the House Un-American Activities Committee. The shunt lever being on the back side and farmers being what they are, in a little hurry, their hands sweaty, late for supper and the shed dark, reduced the odds of hitting the shunt on the first grab. At which point electrical field theory dictates the coil strength of the magneto will surge through the farmer on its way to ground. Forty-thousand volts of Fairbanks and Morse disrupts a farmer's vital signs. Cecil Burns' hired man never was the same after it happened to him and he wet his pants every time he went near a tractor.

The hardest thing for farmers to quit when it came to tractors is the baptisms. A horse wasn't machinery, accordingly lots of horses had names and quite a few earned tombstones. They were

friendly names: Dan, Prince, Andy. Brawny names: Mephistopheles, Caesar, Permafrost. Artful, sublime names: Cleopatra, Victo-
ria, Cutty Sark. Fragile names: Lilac, Daisy, Primrose. The hardest
thing in the new age of tractors was to forego the pet name. Joy-
ous, meaningful, honest names; names that took hold inside the
beast and when you ask Mephistopheles to pull, he'd pull till his
heart broke. All 'cause of that name called and in the mystery of
devotion that horse pulled for all it was worth. No man alive can
see that and not feel love for the beast.

Tractors came from the factory with numbers and alphabet letters; WC, 30-20, the GP. There was not anything living about them
and this failure stalled farming longer than anything before or
since. In due course tractors too got names; like horses they
worked, they balked, they kicked, a few killed their keepers. Farmers came to name their tractors as carefully as they baptized their
horses before. Nothing like Mephistopheles and Geronimo and
Madam Bovary but names never-the-less. There was an Alice,
Roaring John, Moose-brains, Cold Spit, the Holy Inquisition.
Nothing as majestic as horse names but names anyway. Besides,
tractors were only a generation deep in agriculture and had Uncle
Jim's curse on 'em.

The Fence Is Song

It's wrong and I'm gonna admit straight off it's wrong though I do it anyway. The secrecy of the early hours offers sufficient protection to get away with it. I really should try to stop. If any saw me they'd know immediately my purpose, and my community standing would disintegrate before my eyes.

I eavesdrop, I'm a spy, a window peeper, a furtive gleaner of other privacies. It runs in the family. My grandmother slid her fingernail under the telephone receiver, wrapped her ear around it and muffled the mouthpiece with a hot pad. Thus she kept current, steering down the center of the mainstream that was the township.

In the morning woods what still matters is a party-line. From the window I spy on the crow, chickadee, cardinal, whitethroat, song sparrow, oriole, grosbeak, indigo bunting, his majesty of threat the blue jay with a sound video games wish they had. In an hour the finches will claim a share of the wavelength.

It is right to ask if this is noise. I don't think I really know the difference between noise and song. A crow circles the woods and just now has enlisted a companion. Their mutual sound drifts north as they strafe the pine plantation for its owl.

Ornithologists say birdsong is an act of territory. I have no direct reason to suspect ornithologists offer such a claim to satisfy their own pleasures. Just yesterday I engaged a song sparrow in a duel of notes and it took such umbrage at the invasion, it pulled up its gear and charged me. When it comes to tenacity and grit, the Marine Corps ought enlist song sparrows. A double-hung window was over my shoulder, the bird believed his adversary was that sparrow in the window and flung himself at it. The impact knocked him senseless and had I not picked him up to recoup on the clothesline post, the cats would have taken breakfast on the spot. The incident shut me up.

Being a farmboy, I'm grown up with the ridiculous sensation I can talk to anything. There isn't a farmchild in a surplus of cow land who doesn't think he is the equal of Francis of Assisi when it comes to animal correspondence. Ornithologists say this is anthropomorphic, meaning, we are exporting human motivations on the animal world. I do not understand their reluctance toward anthropomorphic arbitration. What is animal and what is human is equidistant from all life forms. I know people who'd benefit with an enhanced attention to anthropomorphism. I build fences and birds build fences; theirs happen to be song. So maybe ornithologists have a point. We ought to be more like birds. The years of my youth would have benefited had I the capacity to fence cows from the neighbor's corn with something other than four strands of cedar. If birds are right about fences, all those miles of wire and staples went for naught. I do know a good war whoop is in all manner a sufficient fence.

Morning noise at the wood edge is more than territory, it's an entire political process. From precinct poll to cabinet appointments, all packaged up in a fit of noise. I don't know whether it's encouraging or an insult to understand all the strut and ruffle of Washington, Madison, and the townhall is within the scale of bird logic.

My point, if I have one and I'm not always so fortunate, is the good health brought on by spewing a little noise. A good dose of bird talk in the morning settles what suicide won't. Somehow being human leads one to think it is necessary to install fences, physical barbs, when metaphysical and syntactical barbs serve just as well and without the bother of fence posts.

I had an uncle who, though married to the same woman the best of fifty years, called her by more names than the woman legally was responsible to. Said it cured him of an itch otherwise persistent. I know what he means 'cause when I was a kid I was regularly condemned to Christian services. The dungeon master was expected to carry on his torture for an hour, not including warm-up and shut-down. By the time it was all over and I emerged from the kirk, I had in my throat a volume of noise that to hold in might have killed me. I let it out.

The preacher had had his chance and whether his fences stood the week remained to be seen. The whole thing is the exact replica of the woods, with the birds all in their pulpits issuing their versions of sanctity. If some collide and the noise rises to a disheveled volume I think it's to be forgiven. Owing that there's no post holes to fill and pack in with an axe handle.

Mowing the Low Pasture

I told my father it was a useless piece of ground. Besides, the low pasture is a bother to mow and rake, bale and haul, besides, it's two miles home. The field is well off the town road and the lane serving it is narrow and overgrown.

Twenty years we argued the low pasture. I wanted to plant it to trees. It's down by the creek, trees would do well. At most it's two and a half acres, this to modern agriculture is really useless. It takes longer to get there than it does to mow it, all for a couple hundred bales. Ridiculous. Plant it to trees. White pine or a grove of reds or sugar maple or let it go to ash by itself. Three years left to its own and there'd be no taking it back.

Pa got sore when I told him the low pasture was useless ground, even if it was. Letting it go wild was worse than dumb to him. A patent sacrilege, an accusation against farming. Letting the low pasture return to woods, how could I even think that way. Cut it, he said. You cut it or I'll cut it, he said with an edge to his voice indicating I ought.

Pa was a dope. What's two hundred more bales of brome grass anyway at a buck each and then only if hay is hard by. I could see the low pasture if it were more alfalfa or red clover. Tain't though and not ever gonna be 'cause the low pasture is where the land

changes from the highland to the low. From there on till nary Bancroft it's black dirt and gumbo, hereabouts called muck.

I told Pa what I really wanted was to dig a pond in the low pasture. Two acres of pond, twelve feet deep with bays and coves and
I'd haul in logs and plant cattails and we'd gain otter and muskrat
and ducks and widgeons. And trout. My own trout. Not the creek's
trout, not Saturday morning fisherman's trout, not the DNR's, not
trout stamp trout. My trout. I'd kill poachers and bury them in the
dry sand at the edge of the hills and they'd corrode so fast the
bones'd dissolve and I'd never get caught.

I thought maybe Pa'd go for the pond idea 'cause he always
talked fishing and never did. He had a trout rod and creel basket
and license and there are trout at ditch eight. You can fish from the
road bridge if you want, right outta the window of the pickup.

Never did. Not him or any decent farmer I ever knew. They
might fish as kids but a thing happened when they became farmers. There wasn't time to fish. Besides, a farmer feels tainted by
public fishing. People who fish are those without an honest attach-
ment to chores. And why is it the best hour for trout is the same
hour God made for milking cows. A farmer who can take Saturday
morning off to fish isn't really a farmer.

Pa died August last, a nice going. A slam-dunk death. Working
in the morning, dinner at noon, dead by bedtime. Surprised me
sorta, which made it marvelous.

I mowed the low pasture last week. Took the long way from the
road, the lane so narrow you can't get above third gear. I borrowed
the neighbor's haybine 'cause he borrowed my welder. We borrow
each other a lot. I already told you it takes longer to get to the low
pasture than to mow it especially with an eight-foot haybine.

I wasn't gonna rake it on Sunday but the day got ruined. She
and I had an argument over clothes. She wanted to wear bib overalls and I wanted to see her in something more delicate than
denim, wanted the shape of her. She said I was being chauvinist

about it. Never used that word on me before and I resented it so went to rake hay in the low pasture. Since the day was ruined it might as well stay ruined.

Took the long way 'cause there ain't a short one. I seen them at the rim of the highland before the lane descends into the muck-lands. Sandhills feeding on hoppers or new grass, they didn't seem to mind the noise of old Allis Chalmers, rattles its cowling pretty bad that one. One did slink off in the rye. Very nearly crawling, if you can imagine a reptile the size of a sandhill crawling.

Raked the hay. Took a dashed long time for such a little field, all that turning. Gawd was it hot, and humid as an armpit. I stopped the tractor under the popple at the creek side of the pasture. There's a spring and watercress and touch-me-nots and cattails and a log acrost. Sat on the log. In the next moment the place became satu-rated with cedar waxwings. The word choice is not in the least metaphorical. There was above me a whole heaven of juvenile waxwings, skinny as green beans, half of them filled with curiosity about me and all of them panting with the heat. I was a good deal less mad than where I started the day. The log acrost displaced most of it and a dose of soft basswood shade did the rest.

She found me there with my shoes off. Wearing a gauze dress, with a bottle of rhubarb wine, two glasses and fresh scones.

I think maybe the low pasture isn't so bad, and maybe I don't ever need trout.

The Recipe

Farming has rules. One of them says that once the farmer has parted company with the breakfast table he does not reenter the house till noon. Unless it is raining. Or he is bleeding. Most farmers, when they do come to the house at noon, pay no overt attention to the meal. Farm wives understand and do not accordingly wait for compliments. There are farmers, it is said, who nap after their noon meal. I will not mention names, but many otherwise competent farmers can not carry on a conversation with a baseball bat during the noon hour. You have to know farmers to understand why.

Despite the previous and nasty comments about semi-conscious farmers who'd eat a cedar shingle like it were toast if served at noon, there is one seasonal departure from the routine. The Fourth of July and the occasion is "the recipe," as traditional and necessary to the Fourth of July as a kid with his finger banged numb from lighting a firecracker with a short fuse.

It is 12:05, the recipe is on the stove. The ingredients simple:

> One quart whole milk
> One half stick butter (like firecrackers on the Fourth of
>   July, we use the real stuff)

124

One pinch salt
Two healthy plugs of pepper
One handful peas (if hands lack size, use both)

and finally,

One hatful potatoes.

This list should be sufficient information for a recipe of peas and potatoes assuming you know how to fly a kitchen stove in the first place. And use a toothpick to jab the potatoes to tell when they are done.

The recipe is complete, but I don't feel right about the Fourth of July without describing some of the recipe's subtleties. Like the milk. I'm not a fan of raw milk except when it comes to an honest try at the recipe. Real milk requires a cow barn, preferably a neighbor's cow barn and a stop in the morning when nobody in their right mind visits a neighbor, particularly a neighbor milking dim-witted cows. A jug of milk at six a.m. on the Fourth of July is worth about what a single malt whisky is worth. I don't know why I think this, other than six a.m. is an awful rotten time to disturb a neighbor. Odds are the neighbor won't take the money and wants to give you the milk. As any who have tried to pay a neighbor for anything know this can nearly turn into a fist fight over who pays whom. Which is kinda ironic in so much as farmers as a group tend to milk a dollar bill for all it's worth and that is why the countenance of old George on the one note looks drained. The point is to either bring hammer and nail the dollar where the farmer can't pull it down and chase you with it, or bring him a peck of new potatoes, which in terms of keeping a neighborhood inflated is worth a good deal more.

About the only problem with a milkhouse at six a.m is the farm dog. Avoid the gait of a salesman. Farm dogs are trained to detect the smell and fine-polish of a salesman, and at six a.m. the dog is at the top of his form. Don't wear clean clothes; an honest layer of gear lube and dirt puts a dog off if maybe you better keep track of his smile.

Another thing, don't enter another man's barn with suddenness. Milk cows with thirty-eight pounds of negative lust towing on their tender ends are surprisingly prone to excitement. They'll go bug-eyed and attempt to jerk their heads out of the stanchions when a stranger is sudden. This in turn doesn't improve the neighborhood. Maybe it would be a good idea to stay entirely clear of the barn until the farmer runs interference for you. By the way, don't plan on getting free right off. Neighborhoods don't pay attention to details of maintaining neighborhoods until the wedding dance and funeral parlor so there's the likelihood once you've engaged, you both are likely to run off at the mouth.

Taters. The reason people started the old peas and potatoes business on the Fourth of July was to get a handle on how the hell the taters are doing. When the farmer can't find a hatful of potatoes come the Fourth of July he is pretty well advised to seek other employment and oughtn't wait till September to start looking. This hasn't changed much now that farmers are outfitted with center-pivots. Peas and potatoes on the Fourth of July is a pretty good judge of how the field is flying. Since I do not raise peas, it means I have to steal them. This, too, has merit in the farm latitudes. A farmer who will steal peas at dawn is the kind of farmer who appreciates dawn for its other qualities. He is also the kind of farmer who endorses the hedgerow standing between the neighbor's field and his own.

Peas are a heck more fun to steal than they are to raise. Besides, it don't hurt a farmer none to keep up on his "marketing" skills. For myself, I favor morning theft. Morning is a good companion for getting a couple pockets full of peas. It warms the heart to steal in the morning. You know you are better for it. Stealing from the neighbor's field at dawn leaves a farmer the more honest the rest of the day. You will wave more often, smile from the pickup 'cause you have a little criminality to adjust for. Does a person good to steal from his neighbor.

    Shuck peas.
    Wash potatoes, but do not peel.
    Simmer peas over low flame, in a small amount of water.
    Cook to texture consistent with your taste.
    Cut potatoes into uniform chunks (small potatoes should be
        boiled whole).
    Add peas and potatoes to milk.
    Add butter.
    Simmer some more.
    Remove from flame and let smell of peas and potatoes fill the
        house.

Being this is the Fourth of July, it is worth taking the noon meal on the front porch or under the tree at the edge of the field, have Mama bring a blanket and pillow. Take a nap. If not, at least hang the cap over your eyes and think things that contentment, neighborliness and a little stealth led you to think. They say the Fourth of July is the national holiday to celebrate our independence. The recipe suggests that for farmers, the Fourth of July is a day to celebrate our dependence on a crop, on the land that yields it, and on each other.

Mud

In all the world there exist but two kinds of mud. Just two, only two, absolutely two. It can be offered and guaranteed that it is so to the far wings of the universe, to where night has been uncut by rude day yet and forever. There as everywhere there are but two, just two, only two, absolutely two kinds of mud.

Mud is either plain or it is not. One ingredient is the difference. No list of accessories, no preambles of doubt and exception, here is total truth. The one variance of Mud is Man.

Philosophers have through the ages gleaned the ripe old histories for clues and indexes. Some say it were, some say it weren't, at half-time they switch sides and uniforms to insure principle, and renew litigation. "Mud," they say and their opposites unsay, "is too close to Man to really be called separate." "Mud," say the suffragettes, "oughta have the vote, whole roads and fields of it should be roped off with flashing lights and barricades at town expense if necessary to insure Mud gets the vote and adequate standing in the realms and glories of Man." "Where, without Mud, would we be; who, just who could we look up to and send to Congress and praise if not for Mud." This party knows of your statues and bronzes, yet are not to be thwarted from their muddled allegiance. Aren't statues and bronzes found to have feet, they ask, 'least toes and calluses and ain't they in the end always clay and isn't clay the right and reasonable product of mud? Clay is but mud that lived the settled life, took up residence and husbandry. It all began with Mud, way back. Farther than even gardens and rumors of gardens. Before there was solid ground or solid morning the whole wide cosmos was one great Mud. Where else could anything as variable and disinclined to obedience as life begin but Mud? Lord, I believe in Mud and just the two kinds. Mud with Man and Mud without. Man himself is inconsequential when compared to Mud. If you've got Mud you've got everything that ever was or is or ever will be.

Mud can think. Most folks don't know Mud can think. And imagine and worry, and besides, Mud can inspire and insult and all at the same try if it wants to. I myself have seen the twentieth century brought to a sloshing, smacking, coagulant halt by Mud. Armies, empires, castles, and seasons, tyrants and bad folk, goblins, saints and categorical sinners; all halted in the full blare of their glory by Mud. Wowed if that ain't handsome as a thing can be and not be worshiped on Sunday morning.

If Mud has a problem, and it's only one, it is that Mud has a hard time with worship. Mud can't see worship as the least very bit necessary. It wouldn't want worship for itself. After all, what difference does it make whether congregations come to your shore and say nice things with their heads bowed? Why should that make omnipotence feel any better? I mean, if you're Mud and know it, no point in taking offense if anyone else knows it or not, or any of the other falderals of destiny, glory, or Oreo cookies enough to last a million billion years. And why have all them folk bent to worship when they could be making useful tidings of themselves? They could be minding chores and kites instead. All what is really necessary is they recognize Mud when they see it. Why build a philosophy around it? All you have to know is nobody can walk across it, not on tip-toe, not on all fours, not in swimming trunks or tall galoshes. Mud sooner or later is gonna getcha. Don't ask color or if it'll go with your shoes.

Yup, only two kinds of Mud. Mud plain and Mud marred. I like Mud plain and travel distances to see whole fields of Mud. Blizzards are nice and corn is pretty but Mud, that is something. Deep? Why nothing is deeper than Mud. Rich? You can't get any richer than forty acres of Mud. A farmer should feel regular proud to have an institution like Mud park itself right where he can up and go and glory at it. Yessiree, in all the world there are but two kinds of Mud. Just two, only two, absolutely two; Mud with and Mud without.

Positive I.D.

It is said farmers are identified by their bib overalls as only farmers wear this apparel cataloged somewhere between the apron and a tool shed. This is untrue; other haphazard sorts besides farmers wear bib overalls. Others have suggested it is the ambush-resistant leather brogues farmers wear; again untrue, others wear shoes equally ridiculous. My cousin Jimmy down the road who's as much a farmer as any and more than most doesn't wear brogies but Keds. According to his wife, six hundred pair per annum; I think the socks are at fault.

What then defines farmers; chambray shirts, flannel perhaps? No, I don't think so, others are similarly apparelled. How about long geeked underwear the kind with a tailgate? I don't believe they even sell those any more being defined pornographic by the Constitutional limits. Or maybe farmers are identified by the distinct pattern of dirt, grease and blood ingrained to their forepaws? Nope.

I know, those caps, those ag-chemical caps farmers wear that are the best way to louse up an environmentalist's day. Plastic caps with plastic fit-em-all head bands, caps that say Ceiba-Geigi, DuPont, Dow, Ortho, Bladdex, Prowl (I rather cherish my Prowl cap but my wife won't let me wear it when I go to town on my own 'cause she thinks it's lecherous). I've seen villagers recoil on sighting these caps. You'd think it said Damnation, War Monger, or Toxic on it instead of something cute like Dow.

Still we are without satisfaction, one conclusive identification that is habeas corpus of a farmer; I was thinking the chances of ever finding a definitive mark of farmers was beyond hope. Thinking pretty serious of giving up my search for a positive I.D. when I happened to attend the Fall Supper and Bazaar held in the cellar of the Liberty Corners Buena Vista Methodist kirk. Ordinarily I'm not a church-goer, kinda leaving that responsibility to my brothers, but I do rouse out for church suppers being as I congratulate myself on being a fair judge at what is a nice religion and what is a true religion. Any as wants to commence theology with chicken and biscuit and sing the hymn of flaky apple pie has my attention and probably my soul.

Anyway, I was in the confines of the kirk and Ladies Aid Society, having a gleeful time with sacrificed chicken when I noticed the last, final, ultimate pedigree of farmers. Farmers have foreheads as no other person, plant, or animal substance have foreheads. Farmers' foreheads glow, they glisten, they incandesce, they phosphor, they occult toward critical mass.

Here in the confines of the Liberty Corner's kirk was what farmers had to finally distinguish themselves: foreheads. Bright, white and glowing foreheads made so by the absence of sun, a tight cap and aided by a hairline in partial or full retreat. This space then on the forehead is where farmers advertise they are the last of the sun and fresh air society. This is not to pretend others don't go outdoors but the agricultural witness is distinctive. Hikers and bikers, golfers and tennis pros spend time outdoors but it is a different outdoors, the dosage isn't the same, the cap isn't pulled on with the same constrictive force. And villagers have time to take the cap off and let the blood circulate in the forehead again, farmers don't. Caps, especially the kind with adjustable plastic bands, are contrived so they get tighter the longer they are worn.

This kills brain cells and tends to keep farmers doing what ever they're doing and producing surplus and maintaining a cheap food policy and nobody knows it's the caps, those sneaky plastic headbands if sized to fit a pecan can smash it into warm pie when set out in a sunny location.

My cousin Harry down the road had about the most premium farm forehead I ever knew. Harry's forehead was like an evening star the way it rioted and spent light, benefiting also from the vast acreage he had available. Added to this, Harry's forehead never saw daylight, and I mean never or as close to rarely I'm only a little lying. Adding ever more to the abuse, Harry was an outdoor farmer, definitely an outdoor farmer. He started a couple hours before dawn and went till something terrible past dark. Harry turned brown as a result, genuine injun brown, a color so rich and uncut Harry coulda changed his race with nobody objecting. His and Hazel's often was considered an interracial marriage.

Meeting Harry head-on somewhere on the townroad down below the first bridge was a wounding experience. You on a tractor, Harry on a tractor. Harry in a good mood. Harry lifting his cap to say hello as you passed and that sudden blindness, like a thermonuclear device exploding three feet before your eyes. Harry's forehead.

Rumor has it they turned off the house lights and saved the electricity when Harry came home and you could tell where Harry was in the house 'cause the glow of his forehead flashed through the windows and seeped underneath the clapboard. Harry had the mark of agriculture pretty bad.

Farm Caps

I have a lucky hat. I realize this is too much honesty for folks, especially when they find out I'm serious. I have a lucky hat, soldered to it since '85 when my previous hat ran out of luck, that the year my dad died and potato prices hit an all-time low for the last thousand.

I switched hats then. I ain't saying any of it was the fault of the hat but it is culpable since it just sat there and did nothing. The law says if you stand by and do nothing when a crime is in progress you are at least half criminal. The law is right.

Religion is in the same business as my hat. Currently I'm a hybrid Zen Buddhist, according to my dead reckoning only a little upstream from Sandy Loam Methodist, neither is very hard paved when it comes to doctrine.

I change religions when the one I'm using fails; I have been told this isn't much of a demonstration of faith. True enough, but it seems the point of religion isn't to make God comfortable but me, it's my hat not his. I already have my next religion picked out—Welsh Hymn Singing, a religion I always wanted to try, where noise is the First Commandment. I've got to learn Welsh though I know most of the tunes already.

Religion reduced to its quintessential itch is nothing more than a lucky hat, but one most folks don't ordinarily change. They wear the same religion their parents wore, which isn't very sanitary. Sooner or later every hat wears out. Like my writing hat. Though it's wearing out, it has served me well, I don't relish changing it. I took up with it many years ago. A friend who baptized me with my first whitewater canoe trip, same guy who dragged me along to watch the sun pry loose of Lake Superior at forty-eight degrees below zero, gave me the fedora his mama's dad wore, a brown, stumpy thing. The hat was run over and spit out a few times already before I even took title. I need a little luck when I write, helps you go where the witchhazel and brush ain't been common walked through 'cept by deer. Sometimes writing is crawling on all fours and groping along in the dark and a lucky hat is appreciated.

My current hat comes from NAPA auto supply, a nice blue with a crisp yellow logo glued to the front. Woven of the finest virgin polypropylene, this hat comes complete with sizing tabs on the back side that permit anyone from Elephant Man to Tom Thumb to think it was custom-made.

Technically my lucky hat is a cap 'cause the porch just comes off the front end and not all the way around. I honestly regret wide brim hats are not more fashionable, a cap really isn't all that much protection. While it does keep the sun off your face a cap has no respect for the ears left flopping around in the open. Ears stick out at least as far as a nose and in my experience ears cook a lot quicker than noses. Caps oughta have little kitchen porches stuck out the side and in this way demonstrate some charity for ears. After awhile a farmer's ears resemble pork cracklins more than they resemble ears.

I've come to appreciate plastic caps. They're cool, indestructible, more often than not free, and if the wind comes up you can adjust the cinch for more traction. This isn't possible with a cloth cap.

I realize village folks are concerned for agriculture when they see farmers wearing caps with DuPont, Dow Chemical, Weedbuster, Bravo, John Deere, and Atrazine stitched on to our frontal lobes. The trepidation is understandable but I want to assure the villager those brand names on the foreheads of farmers mean no more hostility to the world than hats advertising Harley, handguns, or the singing group, Grateful Bitches in Heat.

Don't mean any more than the Guess or Levi branded on the hind quarter of every kid in America or Air Jordan basketball shoes. 'Cept the caps are free and the jeans and basketball shoes are a long ways from free. You can decide who's using whom for yourself. Any time basketball shoes cost more than a fishing car or a pup tent a nation oughta stop and reexamine its values.

Like I say tractor caps are free though sometimes you have to rouse folks. When I go into the local feed and seed I wear the competitor's hat; before I can say ripe rutabagas on rye bread I've a new cap on my head, the old one tore off without subtlety. My sister in-law's old man has a Harvester dealership in northern Minniesorta and I enjoy wearing a John Deere cap in his presence, or a red IH hat when after parts over at Nelsonville. I think I understand better what turns a transvestite's valve stem when I wear the wrong color hat in Deere parts. Quicker than a cat can snag carpet I've got a new cap and a free neck adjustment.

I know farmers who wear tractor caps saying FmHA, or someone's bank or someone's investment company or someone's credit union. You wanna see talons with a death clamp into a skull this is it. Wanna know what it is like to have your face on a Wanted poster look at the wearer of one of these caps, they've got a price on their head and know it. The problem of agriculture is when you distribute in the townships a couple dozen farmers looking like this everyone gets the same worried look after awhile. Same dog-chased, weed-infested look.

I don't suppose having a lucky hat is very bright in this the last set of pins on the bowling alley of the twentieth century. My problem is I don't see luck the same way a villager sees it. For the urban sort luck has no place in reality, what you harvest is the result of loan rates, cash reserves, and market trends. Bad luck is missing the bid for treasury bills or the blip in the bond market or not picketing the School Board when the contract lapsed. The substance involved isn't luck.

Investment bankers don't wear lucky caps 'cause Wall Street and the Grain Exchange don't run on luck. They use charts and graphs and other thinly disguised Ouija boards. They earn money by going trapping for it. They dig a hole, fill it with a big pile of credit and some money and some shiny paint and hope the animal they are trying to lure in their direction smells the money, swallows the credit and gets stuck to the paint. Luck has nothing to do with it, just a pile large enough to attract the animal they are looking for. The same reason machine guns don't need sights on the barrel. Actuaries can tell you why this works.

Mutual funds never get rained on, they might get damp but they don't get rained on. Agriculture doesn't thrive in the same way. In farming if some poor dumb beast doesn't get rained on, flooded out, dehydrated to bone meal, hit with incurable blight or insatiable bugs, then nobody is gonna thrive. All of farming everywhere hinges on bad luck and sometime you gotta take your turn.

Which is why I wear a lucky hat. So far it has done right by me, being insoluble in everything from rain, fertilizer, fumigant, corn dust, dust dust, grasshopper poop, hay chafe, gasoline, prop wash, used burlap, lithium grease... Farm wives who have any sense know they ought not wash the lucky hat, know it might contain the missing mass of the universe or traces of iridium oxide or the last breath of Moses. Washing ruins it. Never mind the sweatband resembles the alkali flats, a farmer is wiser for that hat. Whether he really is doesn't matter as long as he feels this way. Investment bankers know about this only they don't call it luck, they call it a portfolio.

Sometime the luck in my hat is gonna run out and I'm gonna change caps. Might sound cruel but that's the way it is out here.

I know of farmers who won't admit they have a lucky hat, think it is unbecoming in the modern age. But I know and you know they've got one somewhere, maybe behind the seat in the pickup or hanging on a nail in the shed. You can dress farmers in all the three-piece suits and wing-tips you want but if he is a farmer and not idling along on investments he has a lucky hat and knows darn well why. Luck is how the field works. The really scary part is it probably works better this way than if the Department of Agriculture could attach a steering wheel to it. What's scarier yet is there ain't a farmer who doesn't also know the whole dang universe runs the same. Faith then is wearing a lucky hat till the luck runs out, then you know it's your turn, kinda like Zen with an adjustable sweatband.

Road Trees

Road trees are a problem in the townships. According to the town chairmen they come under the jurisdiction of the spring crew. Which happens when a light winter is followed after by an early spring with a surplus in the snowplow account. Surplus at the Town Hall arouses suspicion among the electorate that the mill-rate is set a mite rich. To correct any false impression, the spring crew is deployed to size up the right-of-way, performing as they deem fit. Cutting brush around corners, trimming trees, killing time and any evidence of surplus. Some years they get started right after deer season if the *Farmer's Almanac* so indicates, most likely the job waits till spring since the *Almanac's* been wrong before and running short of plow funds is a heck worse than running a surplus.

Depending on the latent ambition of the crew, a road can go from a middlin' hoot of blacktop down a shaded den to a right-of-way cleared and bushwhacked befitting a four-lane. Changes everything when this is done to a road. Some town roads in the middle of summer have only an hour of actual sunlight, all else in the twilight of thousand-year-old trees huddled on the right-of-way. None of this matters except when the town chair believes the surplus in the plow account looks too blame obvious, combined with a town crew thinking this is their one chance to leave their mark for the next millennium.

Farmers are generally of the opposite persuasion. The road isn't just a way to town but a suit of armor that protects and deflects injury to farm country. A charitable thing is a road since the more brush and overhanging branches a road possesses the slower that smart-aleck dating the neighbor girl is gonna drive his motorcycle or suffer heck. And it is a known fact traveling sales-men will ignore a foreboding road with the nariest glint of light emanating from the other end.

Plain to see what we have here are two opposite inclinations, a test of the divine right of roads on the one hand, and a call to pro-tect and fortify on the other. In the spring the two parties convene, each believing the road is theirs.

Elmer Stenzbinder is the captain of the spring crew on account he drives the town's only Oshkosh. Elmer and I went to school together till he flunked out in tenth grade; been working for the town ever since 'cept for the bean season at the cannery. Elmer owns the longest hitting streak of any of the plow drivers, ain't a snowstorm or mixed flurries Elmer doesn't behead a mailbox. Folks who call the chairman to complain get the standard emergency-vehicle explanation. The hitting streak is only consid-ered broken when the chairman can't explain why the wing should have been in use since there wasn't any snow.

Spring road work is considered pretty nominal as far as the town crew is concerned, not like snowplowing when they're to have the roads open for the milk truck and that means by five a.m. And the Oshkosh ain't worth snot unless it's been idling half an hour and it takes another half for the cab to warm up and you can't get the feel of the hydraulic levers with mittens on, which don't promote the long life of mailboxes. The spring crew is darn nice duty, a well-deserved lean on the shovel while tending a brush fire. The day consists of a leisurely seven a.m. start at brushing, morning break, some more brushing before the noon hour, a little brush then afternoon recess when they pile in the tool truck and bob to the village for doughnuts and coffee.

Elmer and I never were best of friends, a schoolyard wrestle or two about as close as we got. The way I see it, what starts out as road brushing ends up a cordwood fire since it's hard to keep the fire going on sumac alone. Being captain of the guard it's Elmer's decision whether a tree is a hazard to navigation or not. Never mind for seventy years previous it hadn't obstructed anything 'cept an uncomplimentary view across the back side of some field.

I can smell Elmer's fire when he is in range. I have no rational explanation how this is possible though I can tell you it has the same sauerkraut smell his gym locker used to. Doesn't bother me till Elmer and the crew start working this side of Coddington Road or south of the Post. Inside my territory we're bound to have words.

Starts off friendly enough, me reminding him of the time Mrs. Ross stood him in the corner three days running for putting gum in Chester Carmichael's hair, then to make it worse patted it down so the only remedy was to cut a manhole in Chester's scalp. For three days Elmer stood in the corner hand copying the world map and he can still recite countries people with tons of frequent-flier miles never heard of.

Soon enough Elmer and I are arguing whether the tree he cut down was a threat to navigation or not. As brevet captain of the four-wheel Oshkosh, Elmer has the decisive power in the matter and says as much.

I used to argue aesthetics with Elmer. How a road is the more handsome for the tree. How trees benefit the planet and gentle the cold vista on the Big Sandy gone the way of the center pivot. How I once read a book that said trees have legal standing, Elmer saying of course trees have standing else they ain't trees but logs. Elmer is a most inelastic when he is feeling his Oshkosh, though he doesn't know fortissimo from fornication he is willing to define countryside.

Elmer used to make me so mad; you couldn't argue with the guy. He'd just look down his townplow nose and cite the right-of-way width out of the statutes, "thirty-three feet to the center."

I trying to tell him in the pale voice I get when excited how thirty-three feet isn't necessarily a clear span. How in England with more tourists per square foot than anyplace else the roads are narrower than Linda Belmore's hips, roads flanked by stone walls, oak trees the size of silos and people driving Jaguars like bats out of hell. How the whole thing is perfect, people can actually get somewhere, and the road is fair to the eye. None of this touches Elmer except the reference to Linda Belmore's hips.

It got so bad that one time I let out the air on the town dumper when they were gone for afternoon doughnuts. Elmer knew it was me. 'Nother time I clipped the wire on about three miles of snowfence and he had to go back and do it over. Boy was he corked. And when he and his brother came by during gun season like they always do, pretty as ballerinas in their orange parkas, I told him he wasn't welcome to hunt my land any more nor my cousin's neither. Not as I actually asked my cousin.

Next time we met at the Moore Barn he scowled at me while dangling the thick end of the cue stick. Asked straight out what was under my saddle and I told him. He said he thought as much.

At the back pool table that afternoon Elmer and I divided up the world. He agreed to keep to light-duty brushing, cutting doubles and overhangs and I agreed to go after doughnuts if I was headed that way anyhow.

I've got a hedge coming on now that for a couple generations ain't been anything but brush and more brush; when they kept cutting it down to the follicles they only got more brush. Some ten-inch oaks in there already. Last Memorial Day I marked the grave of the Crowfoot babe buried at the roadside during the three-week blizzard of '02, for some reason that seems heroic to me. The spot now has an oak for benediction if you believe such things are necessary. And town crew don't have to put snowfence along that stretch any more and even during a blind white-out running at fifty per across three quarter-sections, that length of road is fine as a summer day.

It has cost me a lot of doughnuts, though.

The Little People

Everybody knows NASA engineers believe in gremlins as are available in all kinds and pedigrees of meanness. If gremlins are all right for science, it is surely kosher for farmers to believe in little people. The Irish are well known for a similar faith, ascribing to every bog and road culvert its sympathetic wee folk. The weekie and smearkle, the bobkin and puny, the cuddle and meowie; some dine on babies, others prefer household trash or lost socks. Ireland is so altogether overcrowded with littles it is difficult to identify which are Irish and which the wee folk.

Yankee agriculture is not yet so overtaken with little people as the Irish, still they are a problem. Science prefers to explain ruin by other causes, though the world is much easier to comprehend if little people are found to blame, not some long-winded Latin disease spread by animals even more invisible who specialize in dirty tricks same as Republicans.

Farmers know the littles are attracted to some crops but not others. Wee folk don't care for rhubarb but will filch asparagus. They have no interest in Brussels sprouts though nibble ripe tomatoes and shake raspberries loose to wear for slippers or condoms or chamberpots.

Wee folk abhor potatoes, especially the weepeeps, a superior strain of littles imported from Ireland who've bothered taties since Sir Walter Raleigh filched the first bushel. Weepeeps are buff-colored and slightly shorter than a #2 lead pencil. For some reason they hate potatoes. It's a known fact they raise potato bugs and in the spring turn loose enormous, baying packs of buggies from their winter quarters in hollow trees, who spend the summer under the green canopy, munching and nibbling. On a still day a farmer can see the leaves of a potato plant wiggle...tis none other than a weepeep running his vexatious hounds up the tater trees. Being so chock-full of terribilating vengeance, as is the Irish predilection, weepeeps carry mildew in their pockets, spilling it on tatie leaves turning slime-ugly overnight, a cursifying if ever there be one. Weepeeps collect the slimy dew and let it ferment, the brew toxic to every living thing save the weepeep who quaff it in noisy little gaggles from acorn caps. Some get wickedly crocked and stumble on the townroad where farmers hope to crush them under the wheels of pickup trucks. This why farmers are seen aimlessly prowling the townroads, in actual practice doing homicidal chores.

The weepeep is related to a Dutch variant called the schnagglenock, known to farmers for its ability to fangle machinery. Blue-eyed and blond, the schnagglenock is equipped with chrome-carbide teeth as can bite through hydraulic lines and suck the juice. They feast on wire cable, insulation, hemp rope, vee-belts and can gnaw a tooth out of a gearbox. They tunnel underground to get at electrical cable and are totally immune to electrocution. Their chief asset is their camouflage, readily mistaken for sheet metal, even tire tread, the facsimile so thorough it includes the bald spot. This explains why farmers are seen beating up an incoherent looking bit of machinery or taking a claw hammer to a sheet metal fender or tire...in reality trying to kill off the schnagglenock as happens to resemble a tire.

Only way to protect any mechanical business from a schnagglenock is to immediately after purchase coat the thing with grease, mud, leaves, chafe, and cow poop. While a schnaggle can lick galvanizing right off the parent metal, they can not tolerate a grease crust or manure splatter. Pickups require a double dose.

The little folk prefer to pick on agriculture and there is nothing the legislature can do to prevent it. In fact some farmers believe legweets have evolved as a specialized taxonomy. These foul-smelling pale cretins dwell in odoriferous marble burrows, allergic to sunlight, thriving on documents seasoned with legalese. Particularly loathsome is their remarkable capacity to write laws. Laws nobody ever heard of as magically appear in the statutes with no trace of ever having passed the legislature. As a result it is impossible for any citizen to remain law-abiding, 'cause there is a law against everything.

Every business has its mix of little folk attempting to infiltrate and ruin them. Hog farmers contend with suffikeets, demon-eyed quirt-tailed rascals with a penchant for suffocating baby pigs and do it with a wink of their green-bean eyes. Sheep farmers have a similar. Wheat and corn farmers are opposed by an even more deadly variety who dwell not in fields where a diligent farmer can squash them, but in the air ducts and dust bins of the Grain Exchange. Known as cheaptweets. Infinitesimally small and sterile, tweets survive on lint and eraser dust. Their goal is to render the price per bushel as close to zero as mathematically possible.

That farmers survive at all in this desperate struggle is less a miracle than the result of a benevolent line of peeps. A variant confused with angels, luck, and genius. Their chief instrument is the miniature hatchet they carry. When a farmer has his jaw set too blame tight to survive, the giggle peep chops it loose. They, the ones who hack notches in the corner of the eyes so a non sequitur smile cures what damn else can.

A favorite weepeep among farmers is the subba cussy; an itsy, bitsy neeked female folk known to dance on a sleeping farmer's forehead. Prance over his eyes, leap across his nose, slide down his cheek, this only when the farmer is taking a nap under a green ash tree. Gotta be ash. Red haired and ample, these otherwise perfect little fems sing lilts in a long absent language. Old farmers report feeling them more than young farmers, massaging their brows with tiny toes, smelling of wild pasture rose, jiggling as a neeked three-inch-tall little folk might.

A farmer has the choice, whether to believe in weepeeps or believe in the random perdition of the free market, the supply and demand mumbo-jumbo. If the Irish know one thing, it is that logic and sensibility are poor entertainments while belief in little folk is more satisfying and smells of pasture rose.

A Family Ground

Lombard Cemetery is on the country road beneath a scattering of hills courtesy of the Wisconsin glaciation. Nothing unusual, a family plot. Enough to hold the profits from the monopoly death has in the business of families. An anticipating piece of ground with room for expansion to the east and north. Around is the obligatory metal fence as required by statute. Whether the wire is to keep the dead in or the living out is uncertain for the parties are generally uncommunicative. We might wager the fence is for the living, an attempt to fence-in dying, imprison it behind rusty wire and posts sledge-hammered in the reluctant stony ground capped with ominous corroded spear points.

The fenced hollow ground of cemeteries makes it easier to forget, reason enough for the fences. Lombard Cemetery has the usual complement of grass and a scattering of stood-up stones, scratched with names. And it has what other grounds don't, a tree of the *pinus strobus* species. An upriver tree common to these parts known for its clear light lumber, easy on saw blades. Among cemetery sextons is the notion trees and proper burying ground don't mix. Trees are messy, scattering leaves and promiscuous shadows, hard on the marriage grass has with cemeteries. Unspoken is a distasteful sense that trees violate the graves.

Some think the white pine is closer to man than other trees. Standing upright the way it does, the way it holds its head and the five green needles that seem long artistic fingers mothers often wish on children. Wishing for musicians instead of thick fingered farmers who can't carry a tune except from a tractor seat. The tree, for these people, is musician enough.

Lombard Cemetery's white pine shares lineage with the empire that was here before the farmer's ground. Hard to tell whether the seed drifted in over the fence, was planted or here before the fence. The tree doesn't crowd the graves, which would indicate it came first, but the tree and the family must have been planted about the same time. The earliest stone is chiseled with the year 1853. Maybe it was a wet year, favorable to seeds, a year when a family would have avoided the cemetery and its fresh earth scab, and chance for a tree to get a start. By the time it was up to their knees it was too late to pull it out, in fear of what its roots might have lay hold to.

The tree and the cemetery have done well. Each prosper on a township fertility. Each show signs of storm. The tree had its top broken off seventy-five or eighty years ago and went from thence double. The family blood was shared with the world; the War of 1812, the brawl between brothers, and the war they thought would end wars. The wars dented the ground here with small noiseless craters. The ground didn't much care what brought them. In due course it took those who lived to become the impassive patriarchs of the front porch with a rocking chair sag. It took children sent by whooping cough and red spots that spread like sunset puddles after a hot rain of fever.

You will hear no complaints from the ground. The tree has come not to pin them down but to define them. The pine has taken up their lives and their voice. A marriage between man, his cant hook, his plow, his bayonetted 30.06, and the many roomed mansion of the tree.

The Lombard tree is a rebel from the rest of the white pine nation. It is the nature of that tribe to be ambitious, height seeking, a climber of stairs, a leaper of fences, an ascender of ladders. An idiot tree that thinks the sky is good ground and wishes to mesh green roots to that blue earth. A haughty tree wishing to be grander, head and shoulders above the rest. The Lombard pine is not following the dictates of its genes. The tree cannot in any honesty be called lofty, rather timid for its kind, if not downright stubby. The wind taught an awful early lesson, instead of a sky ambition, it has gone down, reached under the township skirt and touched the secreted shape of a family buried beneath and beside.

It takes the arms of two to reach around that family tree, one life alone is not sufficient to encompass the girth. Branches that detour from it are thick enough to serve other trees as trunks. Two crowns give it more directions, multiple flight plans and better shade the ground from July's purgatory.

Roots ripple the ground, like water let run over rocks. This flow is quiet. A slow wooden rapids, still it seems headed toward the river. The roots tilt the stones in some kind of contest. Slipped into the ground like grappling hooks sent down to catch the drowned. To eavesdrop on the whispers of this twice fertile ground. The tree knows the stones, the loam, and the bones, a rich ground to curl toes in and touch a coolness to endure long warm summers or long warm wars.

The tree is a fitting memorial to a family. A township kind of people, rooted also in the earth, who like the tree came as frail seed to a strange ground. Both have profited.

Lombard Cemetery is a peaceful place. The near roads carry local traffic; pickup trucks with farm plates gone to market with bull calves, wagonloads of new baled hay, the township plow in winter and an Amish rig on the way to the grocery store. The burying ground hears comfortable sounds.

We wonder what the dead know. Are gravestones periscopes to spy on the subsequent relation? Or did they slip away, whether by vapor or water to the river or by means mysterious. The technique doesn't matter, if only to be partner in the dance, included in the music of a township resurrection.

The tree shades the ground but the shadows spread, pool and linger. Lives beyond jealousy of milking machines, running water, air conditioning, radio, or something besides black wool Sunday suits. Beyond the jealousy of longer lives, penicillin, Sauk vaccine; no longer mad with wares that kidnapped pretty boys. The ground holds a race separate, beyond the roll of drums to stir, who'll not rise to salute, colorblind to flags.

The ground has at last given them the leisure to consider, a dirty kind of business, prone to snide remarks and out-loud laughter. They have their opinions, expressed in the orange prattle of butterflyweed, or the genteel prose of wood anemone. Perhaps their hunger for words is told best with wild strawberry among sand burrs, which in its fashion cuss the grave digger for not saving the black dirt separate. The family is given to speaking in the juicy language of blackberry brambles, the perfumed poetics of pasture rose and lilac, and they howl at the township with the blue throated lupine.

Dying is hard; so removed from living, so alien, so unknowable. We've made the pastures so stony, so sterile, so much more dead Lombard Cemetery doesn't make it seem so bad. A language spoken there that is easy to learn. The Lombard ground is square with the town road, square too with the meridian lines and square with whatever reference lines are out there, no matter the distance.

An Ode to Overalls

Farmers are not poetic animals. The bards come from somewhere but not the farm and every farmer knows why.

Because poetry is frosting on the cookie, poetry is the house with bric-a-brac, a wrap-around porch, maybe a cupola and white pickets. This, according to farmers, what poetry is and has nothing to do with how full the woodshed. Poetry, according to agriculture, is useless as a tail on an angleworm.

However farmers are attentive and reverential to saints and altars no one else finds the least worshipful. Nothing more wows the farmer than a most ordinary occurrence that for some reason is pure amazement. A farmer can admire a vagrant cloud, a lackadaisical sunset, a half-full wedge of geese, a spring of weeds, a drizzle of rain and any of a long list of marvels the standard citizen abandons as entertainment.

Among the wonders farmers find remarkable is the routine attire seen adorning specimens of agriculture. Nary the landsman fails to believe in his heart of hearts bib overalls are one of the seven wonders of the world. Right up on the same shelf as A-bomb, player piano, sneakers, steel plow, the knotter, and the potato seed cutter.

Overalls go by different names, variable as the regions of the country. Some call 'em bibs, others call 'em overalls, and a litany follows; o'ralls, baggies, field duds, spud duds, barn duds, farmer clothes, ag zoots and zacks. While it is true bib overalls are not solely the costume of farmers, they have for the purpose of type-casting become the exclusive kit of agribusiness, especially the end of the endeavor that is more aggravation and plain busy than it is business.

Who exactly invented bib overalls is lost among the other mysteries, the same as what Salome did with the head of John the Baptist after she took the platter. We probably don't really care to know anyway, least not at suppertime. Some farmers believe overalls were designed by God and were found hanging on a thornapple tree alongside the fig leaf the morning after the auction of the farm on Eden Road. An honest cynic objects to this predestined cant, knowing overalls were no more designed by God than is the four-cylinder Holstein. Never mind they both have blessed utility written all over them. Meaning the invention is more from humankind looking for a shortcut than the result of divine providence. God may well have designed the gambrel barn but it was a farmer with a dose of the hurry-harries who invented the pole shed.

Overalls are made for one thing and one thing only. Doing anything else in bibs but this ought leave a person feeling funny. Same as playing jump-rope in a cemetery. Bibs are for working. They are not for lounging, sailing, playing basketball, golfing, or any of the other exercises villagers have contrived as artificial sweat.

Farmers who consider themselves and their vocation modern do not wear bibs. Overalls do not go well with a suit coat and tie although they aren't so bad with Harris tweed. Bankers, seed dealers, and extension agents do not admire a farmer in bibs as sincerely as a farmer in slacks and baseball cap. This is the way things are. The nun forsakes the habit, the priest wears a jogging suit, and the farmer who wishes to be thought modern must forsake overalls. Never mind this same practitioner wears blue-jeans so tight as to bring on falsetto and pockets so marginal a jackknife overwhelms them. If nails, pliers, or a hammer are required he straps on an apron, which adds nothing to the manly appearance.

The intent here is to praise bib overalls. To so hoist them up the flag pole of farmerkind that all shall know bibs as the faithful and local companion of the agricult.

The public rumor about overalls is cruel and mischievous. They are not the cheapest way to clothe a person. The loincloth is, the kilt is second, bibs are third. It is true Mark Twain doubted the morality of bib overalls, on account a person can exit bibs several times faster than they can exit a loincloth.

When it comes to clothing it is no accident bib overalls are the exact median between total nudity and a suit of armor. Every farmer knows bibs are a lot closer to an exoskeleton than they are to quaint custom of dress, how on a humid July afternoon of piling hay in the barn of damnation, the only reason the farmer is still standing erect are his overalls. The same is true of storms, muds, and blizzards, that otherwise would dissolve the farmer and convey his salt to the sea, were not the bibs the more insoluble of the two.

Were self-preservation the only thing bibs had to offer agriculture they still wouldn't be the costume of the vocation. Because farmers, as everyone knows, have little interest in self-preservation. The reason bibs are the anthem of husbandry from Maine to the Wabush, from the Brule to the Rio Grande is because bibs fulfill the three premium needs of agriculture. Shed, pickup, and toolbox. All supplied by a two-buckle appliance. In fact bibs are not one shed or one pickup truck only, or toolbox, but a complete set of sheds, pickups, and toolboxes, none of which require a license plate or registration fee. Meaning pockets. Bibs have a monopoly of pockets.

The right front pants pocket is more badger hole than it is pocket. Capable of swallowing an entire twelve inch crescent wrench and leave no evidence of the tool or the seriousness of the breakdown. It will also conceal a sectioned fly rod, pup tent, trolling motor, hammock, or the large print version of the King James.

Below this pocket reside two others, both pliers pockets. Why two? 'Cause one might get lost. Behind is the hip pocket, as voluminous as its neighbor, for a pair of gloves, in fact two pairs, and an afternoon's worth of fence staples.

Left leg, another badger hole just as deep as its sibling. Farmers lose stuff in those pockets and there are in farmtowns housekeepers who'd rather burn a pair of bibs that attempt to wash the things. Smart wives let the garment rattle around in the washing machine for awhile to kill off the aliens spawned in the depths of the pocket. Aliens born of the random marriage between barb wire, wood screw, cough syrup, and eight penny nail.

Below is the hammer loop, heir to the six-gun and holster, feeling that good against the leg. The hammer banging against thigh makes a person feel useful whether they actually are or not. This in turn allows farmers to believe they can fight off any invaders, the old sword and buckler sensation. All from a hammer and pocketful of nails.

If every farmstead is plagued by a shed too many. If farmers to the discerning public have an urgent reckless way with board and batten. This hammer loop below the left front pocket is the cause. It is also the favored target of dogs who go for the loop and hang on with a grin. Doing little for the long life of the garment or the intended trajectory of the wearer.

Hip pocket left behind, more garbage can than pocket. Herein go oil rag, enough new potatoes for supper, a baby chicken, a half dozen ears of sweet corn. Not only is there room for everything but it is possible to sit on the contents without crushing, suffocating or even feeling them.

What makes bib overalls about the best article of clothing the world has ever witnessed except maybe the grass skirt is the bib and its complication of pockets. Store clerks hate bib overalls with a passion and the way a customer frisks himself in public. Fore-

boding to think what the guy might pull out believing it feels like
a coin purse. Disrupts business and assaults those of refined taste.

In the bib the farmer keeps his library. The seed corn notebook
that doubles as an account ledger and a personal journal. This is
his filing cabinet, the list for town, the wiring diagram of a motor,
a pocket watch, a letter from Texas, the remains of a flower, one
briar pipe, a mixture reminiscent of tobacco, a pretty feather found
in the pasture tank, and a photo of a red-haired daughter.

In the farmships it is widely known that farmers do not possess
souls, bib overalls do, and this why farmers wear them. This tent
reveals all their habits. If the man chews, the ghost moon shows
through the bib. If he takes pipe, the stem protrudes. Not only is
the bib their soul but it is glass and displays all what is to be
known. Religion is ciphered by the pale patch of repetition where
the thumbs backed against the chest in an earnest first-light prayer
where none saw but God. If he was free thinker that church
showed, fish hooks and trout flies snagged in the thread. There are
farmers who have a custom of carrying stone. A lucky stone. The
one they found as a kid, found in new ploughing, a stone curious
in shape, whether maiden or bird they can't say. The stone is a natural rosary the man can tumble in his worry, carried for luck, if
farmers have such. The bib is where the man carries home a pine
cone or the gopher's jawbone found by the road, blue as a Ford
tractor it was. Kids learned to search the bib for candy and pillow
packs of BBs and marbles and salesman's pencils.

The last pocket? Front and center three buttons, the pocket
snickered about. In the farmships known as the Saturday night
pocket or grandpa's retirement plan, this more than enough said.

Bib overalls were the armor to what the farm knew of cru-
sades. A pair of my father's overalls hang from a white-washed
timber in the empty cow barn. I do not know why they are still
there, the man gone to another ground. Of what farming is, the
overalls seem memorial enough. A wren left a nest in the front

pocket last summer. The wind through the dutch door shakes them as if in the act of dressing. I have the feeling I should drive a nail through the overalls to hold them still. Maybe it's just too many Dracula movies...

Lengthwise and Across

F armers all have similar tales and when the chance permits we wag them for our own satisfaction and contentment. The reader will recognize the tale, the fur may vary but the stripe is about the same. Put a farmer on a barstool and sooner or later the tale emerges and winds around the stand, a tale of how it was in the old days. Note the expression. There is no farmer of any pride or longevity, with a length of family rope, who does not have the scent of the old days about him. Anything at all can set it off and the farmer becomes a lyric voice. His face flushed with the memory and enchantment of how it was, once.

Seed cutting. When the white farmhouse on the sand-end of the marsh road took up potatoes, the method of cutting seed had not varied for a century. It was an ashboard, the same ashboard, same butcher knife stuck through the slot in all that hundred years of potatoes.

Like many sand farms, the one of my nativity grew potatoes sporadically. The spud crop fitted with other crops, and of course those price fluctuations produce fits. After the disastrous years of the early and mid-thirties when potato prices hit fabled lows of fifteen cents delivered in Waupaca, the farm, with the snit of a jilted lover, went to dairy and did not return to commercial potato acreage for a generation. When we did, it was with the same pestilential ashboard, the one with the butcher knife stuck in the slot.

The idea behind this advanced bit of technology was to hold the board on your lap, pinch the handle of the knife between your knees and with a scrub-board motion, cut the potato first lengthwise, then across. It was a task, as any who can recall, perpetrating a distinct and odious tedium. A tedium so intense and unremitting it tended to insure that those offspring who were raised in the habit of potato production did not choose it as a career. One potato at a time, sliced lengthwise so thin and keen the potato whispered through it without effect. It was after all the best knife on the place, one of those beaten Japanese blades folded and hammered by a hunchbacked Buddhist monk to an edge so fine it'd cut a water molecule in half. How this exotic blade came to reside on the sand end of an unnamed town road is unknown, that it cut seed potatoes for the better two generations is true enough. Sleek as sin in silk stockings was that knife protruding out the ashboard. The edge beaten so fine, light shone through it. A blade to raise the IQ of farmboys who were pretty darn smart to begin with, lengthwise and across, lengthwise and across.

The central satisfaction of cutting seed potatoes was sitting down. The board on the lap, the knife held between the knees, lengthwise and across. The juice drained off the end of the board and down the pantleg, in turn inspiring the advanced technology of a potato sack over the knees. So the sack got wet before the pantlegs did. This was a major improvement. Of course it only delayed the inevitable wet pants but thinned out the discomfort so the seed cutter got used to the damp gradually and so paid the event little attention. This was same format of protection used in many farm activities, an attempt to water down the side-effects so that by the time the practitioner realized what was happening, it was too late, and any improvement didn't matter. In fact, improving the situation merely demonstrated how darn uncomfortable you were in the first place.

The place chosen to cut seed potatoes always suffered the same conditions. No matter the farm was in Antigo, Rice Lake, the rocky shore of Custer, or the sand dunes of Plover, every tater farmer cut seed potatoes in the same, exact, absolutely equal kind of place.

Condition number one; the seed cutting room had to be, by law, unheated. Note here, the seed cutter is sitting. Not standing, not moving his feet, but sitting in one self-same frozen spot with potato juice dripping down his pantleg. The place slightly more clammy than the third underbasement in the Tower of London where the blood from beheading collected and pooled. There was a time when a tater farmer did not feel wise and wonderful if he had not planted potatoes by Good Friday. Never mind Easter is hitched to the moon and flies over snowbank as easily as warm ground. The farmer was obligated to commence cutting seed in the aforementioned tatie bin, his prospects aimed at Good Friday, and three feet of snow against the shed door.

Condition number two; no seed cutting area was supplied with what the modern would describe as adequate lighting. Light was thought hazardous to potatoes, besides, there was a light bulb in the fixture over by the cellar door. So there's plenty of light. Besides, dimness reinforced the seed cutter's concentration. Lengthwise and across. Lengthwise and across. That molecule-splitting blade catching just enough light to tell where it is. Keep the board steady and the motion routine, lengthwise and across. See, you don't need light do you?

Condition three; ventilation. Dracula would have loved the potato bin down there at the bottom of the stone-faced cellar. Here was a dank to thrill Transylvania, a musty, glued-together smell of potato skins, dirt, mold, and mouse droppings. No one knew then potatoes were respiring and the potato cellar was filled with exhaled carbon dioxide the same as if a slow breathing beast were sequestered in the cellar. What seed cutter did not feel drugged, his hand turning that tinge of blue, more lavender actually. Lengthwise and across.

Condition four; endurance. What farmkid did not understand the awful sentence of seed cutting, the miserable justice of it all? Even felons of homicidal crimes had kinder fates than twenty acres worth of seed potatoes. Lengthwise and across. One potato at a time and twenty acres is cruel and unusual, not even counting the Japanese edge sticking through the slot.

Condition five; boredom. We did not know then the term "child abuse." If we had, the potato would have become extinct. Lengthwise and across. The kid in the tater bin knew what all slaves of empire-builders know. Either do yourself the favor of dying right away or live long enough to gain vengeance. Lengthwise and across. We began plotting at an early age. Lengthwise and across. First thing we'll do is get rid of the demon gloom. A forty watt lightbulb, even seventy-five watt, maybe it would give off some heat. Lengthwise and across. And a radio, yeah a radio, whenever they invent one with any kind of reception twelve feet underground. Lengthwise and across. And then a machine, yeah a machine to cut seed potatoes. Wow, can you imagine such a machine? Not really. It will never happen. Impossible. It'd ruin agriculture and child rearing. Lengthwise and across. Still, the children of Tuberosa Rex thought and thought. If only there was a way. Lengthwise and across. Some dream machine with levers and cogs and guillotines, slicers and dicers and pieces with eyes. Lengthwise and across. Lengthwise and across.

Part of all potato farmers is yet in the tatie bin, back there somewhere in the dim, still cutting seed. Lengthwise and across. And dreaming of new ways and sometimes, horror of horrors, dreaming of old. Lengthwise and across. Lengthwise and across.

Blackberry Liberation
and Doghole August

tevens Point Daily Journal, January 30, 1904: "Early last
week a girl about twenty years old put in an appearance at
Junction City dressed in men's clothes. For several days she
hung around one of the saloons of that village and on the streets
drinking and smoking (and wearing men's clothes)...Finally, however, her presence became so obnoxious to the good people of the
village that Deputy Sheriff Grasshorn arrested her and brought her
to Stevens Point..."

The paper reported the girl was later released to her liberty
since no warrant was issued for her arrest whereupon she sought
refuge in "one of the South Side resorts"...this despite her vulgar
and shocking costume.

When I was a kid, not all that long ago, women and females
did not wear pants, neither Levis, bibs, shorts, hot pants, cutoffs,
dungarees, biking tights. If a woman wished to crowd morality
and arouse something more revolutionary than idle gossip, she
only needed to be seen wearing men's pants. At the time it was
considered pretty much an admission of semi-harlotry.

With such a fence provided, women who were serious about
their reputations did not wear pants, it simply wasn't done except
by the acrimonious, the deranged or by the loose category of

females as dwelt out west toward Junction City. Why women were
denied pants was less apparent though it really didn't matter as
long as it wasn't done and when something isn't done for a long
enough time, not doing it takes on moral posture any healthy and
decent person can feel in their rumen.

I was a kid back then when if a person wore a dress they were
a female and if they wore trousers, they were a male. Nobody in
those privileged times had any confusion about sexual identity: if
you couldn't remember which bathroom to aim at one glance at
your clothes provided a quick reference. This was way back when
gay meant a mood of frivolity, queer meant something strange, and
transvestites were zoo animals.

When I was a kid back in the Age of Chevrolet a person's sexual identity was observable from a quarter mile away, either it
was trousers or a dress with no half measures. Being a kid was
awful easy.

When you wanted to draw a picture of a woman the symbol
required was an abbreviated tent hung on the person's hips.
Granted, even back then this figure might have indicated a Scotsman wearing a kilt but kilts occurred so rarely in the township it
was discounted, except as a rumored tradition among my former
relations who reputedly wore kilts. But this was way back in the
days of Charlie Rice who ran a tavern on the banks of the Plover
and John Baptist DuBay was his first next-over neighbor, meaning
there was more empty space then. A person can wear what they
want with or without society's approval given enough empty space,
including the transvestite costumary called a kilt. Sexual identity
was either the dress for womenfolk or a polluted Scotsman, and
trousers indicating menfolk. There weren't any gays, queers, dukes,
dykes, wingdams, transvestites, Baby Ms. surrogate this, donor
that...everything was hard shell, no soft serve sexual identities...a
person either was a male or female, if occasionally Scots.

Those were innocent times. Men didn't hold hands and

wouldna been caught dead holding hands with another man unless they were actively pumping a handshake. Nobody would have put a bumper sticker on a car saying "Have you hugged your kid today?" Parents didn't hug kids back then except overweight aunts who hugged just to hear a kid's bones crack.

Now folks hug for all kinds of therapeutic reasons, hug anytime they want, men included, and women can wear pants even if wearing a kilt is still for the foolhardy.

The rule of women in trousers had one exception, blackberryin'. Those who know blackberries understand it is an unkind vegetation. Biology has never been more profane and hostile than blackberry cane: it came equipped with dagger, switchblade, stiletto, and skein dhu. Picking blackberries required about the same courage as facing live ammunition, required a clotting blood type and the small benefits of personal armament, this why Mama wore pants.

To a kid raised under the implications of sexual identity directly attached to the garment, seeing my mother and grandmother in trousers and men's white shirts with the intent to go berrying was not only remarkable, it was confounding. Apparently I had not realized the shape of woman existed independent of the dress. I was surprised my mother had legs that ran full-length and didn't end just above the knee as the dress suggested. Up to this point I had a pretty good idea why females couldn't run worth spit, because they didn't have the full-length ambulatory to do so. The remainder of the female volume was in my imagination devoted to perpetuation of the species.

I had made the mistake of assuming a logical reason existed for women in dresses and menfolk in trousers. After all threshing machines weren't voluminous for nothing, neither are barns, silos, granaries; all have reasons for their shape. So I assumed females wore dresses because their biology required it. At the time I was not interested in finding out why, no more than I was about to find out how a threshing machine worked by sticking my head in one. Puberty was longer back then compared to the modern age because back then females were not to be messed with.

Blackberries and drought do not mix, neither is rain every other day. Blackberries are not only hostile vegetation, they're darn persnickety. Add to this that they ripen in the middle of dog-awful August about the same time as white oats and second crop of alfalfa and if it got any hotter the barn'd melt, and every kind of cannibal fly is sucking blood right out of you.

This exactly when Whittaker's woods came ripe, ripe and sacred with blackberries, so overflowing with blackberries you could smell the purple. When the sunlight through a blackberry woods took on a sweet, lurid coloration. All account of the black-berries hanging like a treasure trove with translucent rubies.

Whittaker's woods was the best picking around 'cause the tor-nado of '38 smashed the woods. Ruin always did favor blackber-ries. Same thing on the backside of the moraine where blackberries grow terrifying among boulders big as a house, this where every snake in the township retreats to last out the dog month of August.

It was blackberries that brought Mama to trousers. By August the summer heat had finally soaked through the farmhouse and there were nights oat chafe wouldn't wash off even if you used gunpowder for soap. Nights so blame thick the bed stuck to you and you couldn't roll over without turning the whole bed after you. Nights I'd slip out the upstairs window and sleep under the porch with the dog and any spiders as wanted 'cause it was some cooler there.

Mama in trousers spoilt my rendition of the female machinery. They weren't voluminous combines after all but sleek as deer and probably could run if they had a lesson or two.

The reason I'm telling you this is Mama never marched in a feminist parade, never burned her bra, but she did wear trousers when August came ripe, and once that was liberation enough.

Blackberry liberation.

There were farmers who kept blackberry woods and those who didn't. Some did it for pie, some for jam, for others maybe it was accidental. For some I think it was for trousers and womenfolk getting full-length legs. This in the time when I was a kid and the high school didn't have girls on the swim team or girls basketball...but there were farmers who knew better and kept a blackberry woods.

The Popple Grove

The popple has few admirers. Popple trees are not planted on city boulevards, neither in front yards or national parks; popple is not sufficiently dignified. Bankers will not give popple a car loan—even for a used car—popple can not enter public restaurants, popple is useless, bare-foot, no-account, good-for-nothing. Popple has a loitering personality. The tree is a gang member, it is more quackgrass than tree.

Popple is what rural folks call the vegetation, presumably a corruption of an earlier epithet. The tree never was popular anywhere. Calling an unpopular tree popular is crude humor and country people are constantly upbraided for smearing the perfectly good pejorative to popple. Calling the tree popular is like calling Woody Allen's movies funny; intellectually stimulating, but not funny.

It could be worse. The correct name for popple is aspen. It doesn't take strenuous tipping at a country tavern to make a rude hook from that word.

Popple's chief attribute is its total absence of integrity. You can not insult a popple. No ground is so poor that popple will not, given the opportunity, advance a generation across it. No other tree is so disrespectful to the prospects of its offspring. Popple will spend seed on a ground that couldn't grow dirt much less trees.

Leave a field unattended for a year and by the following summer popple are hanging around the street corners talking dirty. By
the second year it's standing-room-only with the neighborhood
shot to hell and not a high school diploma in sight.

Popple is a welfare tree. It will not seek higher education, will
not study the French philosophers or watch "Casablanca" or any
movie in black and white. Nothing can devalue a neighborhood
faster than popple. All the college-educated trees move out
because they can not understand the jive of popple. Popple never
mows the front yard, the tree is unkempt and given to clutter, and
popple has too many kids.

The first thing a good forester does is tie the tubes of the popple, kill off the rougher looking kids and get the rest to study alge-
bra. It's blame difficult to make something of popple, the tree just
doesn't want to work. Its grain is full of comic books and the car
magazines. It can not discuss world affairs. Popple is praised too
much when it is called good-for-nothing.

My father hated popple, a smooth and deliberate hate it was,
pure as the driven snow. No finer hate could you find than how Pa
felt toward popple. On a hot summer afternoon when he couldn't
think of anything else for us kids to wage at, he sent us to chop out
the popple from the back-pasture.

There is no more demented chore than chopping popple. After
the first whack the axe loses its edge, after the second it becomes a
blunt object. After the third, raw vocabulary is all that remains;
killing popple is more linguistics than chopping.

It was in a corner of the back-pasture that popple eradication
had gone undone. The popple there had a head start and no amount
of pulling, chopping, or verbalization was gonna upset the grove.

The popple grove was all you could see of the low pasture
from the barn. In the spring the mustachioed buds resembled from
a distance smoke drifting among the branches, signal popple was
making camp. This, before any other tree had even turned over

from its dark winter slumber.

By the time the rest of the woods—the ash, the oak, the maples and tamarack—were looking for their underclothes, the popple had already put in a couple weeks of loitering. Dressed up and talking asocially, wearing what a proper tree won't be seen dead in. Long before the present human generation espoused the wearing of mini skirts and neon colors, popple has worn an electric wardrobe. Other trees have coloration, popple has voltage. The leaves of the popple grove were a corona of excited ions, they lit up the low pasture amongst a dark and somber spring. From the barn you could see it, spangling like a fuse on a siege cannon.

Autumn is just another popple theater, no other tree dies with so much operatic dessert. Yellow is only an estimate of the color, the popple grove was a bubble of incandescence. Its brilliance required a welder's mask to look at directly, as if a piece of the sun had fallen among the trees and ignited every leaf.

The only time the popple grove was any use at all was during summer's armpit. That week or two when the thermometer got stuck on the ladder and like a kid was too scared to climb down. Nights when the Amazon jungle complete with the smell of wild bananas shifted north in malevolent Doppler. The air humid as a crowded funeral parlor, a sticky-glue kind of heat that embalmed people in their pajamas. You could no more fall asleep than an amorous tomcat.

Weren't a place fit for habitation this side of the North Pole with exception of farms as hadn't abandoned the icehouse. So dashed awful whole families retired to the potato cellar as they were that deep and that cold. Lore said you could get twelve-gauge rheumatism doing that, which prevented some from trying.

The only other salvation of a summer night humid as a buffalo stomach was the popple grove. Soon as we finished supper we lit out. Equipped with no more accessory than a feather pillow and torn quilt, like safari porters, off to the back-pasture.

In the grove the grass stood waist high, this we promptly flattened without effort. On the wreckage we deployed the quilts and pillows.

It wasn't exactly the coolness of the popple grove we were after as much as the sound of the leaves. Never mind there wasn't a loose breath of air in the entire township. Notwithstanding smoke rose straight into the ionosphere, every leaf in that grove was fluttering. Jiggled by what energy we couldn't guess, the resulting sound the exact of a brook flowing over a patch of trout water. A gurgling, joyful noise. You needed only to hear it and be cooled.

It was of the popple the Psalms spoke, "...a tree planted by the rivers of water...." Cool trees in over-heated fields, in this is the comfort of the Lord.

When I was a kid there were preachers in the pulpit of the Liberty Corners kirk who believed Psalms was full-length metaphorical. They had never been to the popple grove and known the Psalm of refreshment. Never lain on the grass and heard the voice of a tree comfort a fevered world, a cooling breeze where no wind was. In the morning we were rolled deliciously in our quilts, wrapped in and sung over. The singing cool from a good-for-nothing tree. This at a time when only the taverns were air-conditioned and we temperance methodists, with only a tree to save us. Saved by the popple grove and the night so very, very cool.

Tits

The failure of this subject to enjoy a place in literature is the fault of the word. Every farmkid knows tits is one thing one place and another thing somewhere else. In the barn, tits are not only acceptable language, they are required. Tits are the reason for milk cows. To call them udders, flanges, lugs, teets, penduncles, posterns, mammaries, spikes, totosh, lactative peninsulas is too much elegance, like wearing a tuxedo to a barn raisin'. So cows have tits and nothing but tits.

Beyond the barn this literary order reversed, no mention of tits is allowed except by the dictionary handles. The church, Sunday School, and schoolroom all follow the udder rule which made it difficult on farmkids who had to switch languages depending on the circumstance. To talk about udders at the feedmill invited ridicule but in school it reflected positively on a kid's linguistic skills. In the barn speaking in terms of udders and flanges was plain uppity, like wearing rubber gloves to dress a chicken, like you are afraid to touch guts.

None of this really matters but for the occasional farmkid whom the fates have immersed in the sociological dimensions of the cow tribe. I was raised in the circumstance of this muddled morality as were a couple dozen others. Raised within the moral hygiene of the milch cow to whom previous generations of my kind had been devoted. I did however escape one terrible episode in the kingdom of lactation namely milking by hand. This was my father's fate and as awful fates go, that was close enough. I witnessed firsthand the effects of milking by hand, the result of a lifetime of pulling tits. My father's hands were so completely transformed by the daily chore that work gloves matched to his body didn't fit his hands, instead he wore gloves three sizes in advance of the rest of him. Twice daily had so altered his hands they resembled Virginia hams hanging from his shirt sleeves.

This all changed when rural electrification brought power to the townships. If others entertained a variety of uses for the new resource, my father had but one hope. He didn't honestly mind kerosene lights, the arc welder could wait, same for window fans, radios, washing tubs, water pumps, hot water, and electric toasters. What he desperately wanted was salvation from the chore of eventide and morning. Deliverance from the "old squeeze," that educated rolling grip dairy farmers had so trained to their hands. Left to their own devices his hands followed this incipient motion, they milked when he slept and sat in the semi-hypnotic state of the church pew. When holding hands with my mother and his mind relaxed, his hands began. They seldom held hands. Thus the single, most intoxicating thrill of R.E.A. was not augers and conveyors, not running water and electric lights, it was the vacuum pump.

For untold centuries farmers have sought release from milking, the most egregious of chores. Above all others this stood out as the most awful to be performed twice a day by mortal man. Inventors of its replacement had run the gamut of devices fueled by the broad sympathy for relief. All kinds of devices were put forward to gain, encourage or extract lactation from cows. Some promised ease and rapid removal but killed the cow. They were driven by wind power, by treadmills harnessed to children, horses and dogs. They squeezed, flattened, exerted, pulled, pried, nibbled, gnawed and other equally inappropriate therapies to withdraw milk from the bovine. All failed including the machine built from the drawings of Leonardo da Vinci. One example developed in Bridgeport, Maine, collapsed an entire barn including a mow of loose timothy on a group of spectators gathered for the experiment. Luckily the inventor himself was killed outright.

Persons of all reputations took up the challenge to find the complete mechanical milker. Steam power was employed on countless variations. One invention by a female inventor from Ohio used steam-driven pistons disguised as calves that were placed on the cow and once the engine had come to pressure and the valve was thrown open, the pistons descended withdrawing the entire milk supply in one clean stroke. It worked marvelously except for one flaw, the cow never milked again as the mechanical calf had removed her biological underpinnings.

Two kids from Minnesota developed a bicycle-driven contraption that employed mechanical hands to squeeze the milk out between shaped basswood forms. To milk one cow required twenty-two miles worth of pedaling. Still they kept trying; water power, wind motors, steam in hundreds of variations; nothing seemed to work except the traditional. It was about here a renowned inventor of home improvement devices, none of which survive including his patented automatic letter licker or pancake flipper, made an attempt at a milking machine. It was he who also invented a steam-powered weathervane, a treatment for garden weeds, mechanical butter churn that doubled as a shoe buffer and laundry aid. He attempted vacuum-assisted wart remover that when applied to an affected area, withdrew the oxygen supply over the wart and reduced the skin to such a hostile condition warts naturally abandoned the spot. The device had, he believed, wide application as a homeopathic device. The contraption was an abiding and dismal failure. Except. Except for an accidental application of his wart remover to a cow on a farm near Peoria, Illinois.

Work? It was absolutely stupendous. For twenty-thousand years, Anglo-Saxons and Huns, Goths and Hindus had searched for this very passage, the precise instrument in lieu of milking by hand. The wart remover was the exact duplication of how the human hand approached and gripped the lugs of bovines and it milked Jerseys as easily as Holsteins, Guernseys, Brahma, French yellows, Freislands, American bison, musk ox, and all with nothing more than a surplus vacuum pump or engine manifold.

Hence the vacuum milker was the first instrument of electrification my father brought to the homestead, so sure was he the practice would prove effective he hung his milking stool on a nail behind the silo door and from there it did not move in the next generation. That milking stool was never honored, neither painted nor cleaned of cobwebs, it was not deemed fit to take down from its nail for the sake of an antique sentiment. To make double sure it wasn't, the nail was crimped over and duly folded into the beam. And hand milking was nailed forever behind the silo room door and don't anybody ever think of reviving it even for fun.

This brings dairy history to the threshold as I knew it and the incident for which the milking machine proved useless. It was through this I learned to milk by hand so I could sincerely hate it. The exception to the rule of machine milking was the new heifer, for all practical purposes a cow except for the fitting of the milking machine to her parts. Why this event did not make its way into rodeo competitions I have never understood. It is at least as dangerous as trying to ride a wild horse for the first time. The difference is the starting position. On the horse the rider starts out on top and ends up on the bottom, in milking heifers the participant starts out under the cow and things deteriorate from there.

For those who do not yet understand, a bit of remedial education. Understand a heifer is less a cow than a dry-land shark. A naturally wild animal that for the two years previous has enjoyed the pleasures of the back pasture and woodlot, its life sweeping from one zeal to the next. The heifer, being on semi-friendly terms with the farmer, had submitted to fertilization if not artificially served then through an enlisted resource. Most heifers accept this as one more wilderness function, none realize the forces now unleashed will lead to the corruption of every freedom they had to this point. Her body sleek as a lioness, capable of leaps and prodigious velocities now vehemently turned against her. Her belly swollen she no longer feels the zest of former days and most importantly, most tragically, she is crippled. Lamed and hobbled by as cancerous a growth as ever visited biology. A swelling of tissue and gland that robbed her of her wild station. A traveling case the size of a golf bag with four deliberate oblongs protruding from her tender self that grew and distended and in the space of ten months changed her from the sleek huntress into a buxom dowager.

Here began the tit wars as I knew them, the bringing to fold of this new cow who on freshening had yet to be taught barn discipline. Here stood I and every barn bairn, as tutor to the yet pagan heifer, alone with her and her resentment. For her part she smoldered in her stanchion. Vengeance glistened in her eye as the choreboy approached with the patent, stainless steel, vacuum-propelled wart-remover.

A cow is fitted as everyone understands with a rudimentary set of muscles for locomotion. This bone-red meat relationship is sufficient to all needs, but evolution overwrought the cow. It did not stop at locomotion, rather continued the perfection of muscle and bone so that a standard cow is better likened to a booster rocket in animate form. When John Thomas cleared the seven foot mark in the high jump in 1960 a cow had already held the mark for twelve million years. Same with broad jump, the mile run, and the steeplechase. John Glenn beat bovines into orbit only through the benefit of artificial atmosphere. So it is this natural propellant is stored within inches of the very kid now detailed to acquaint the heifer with her twice-a-day allegiance. Tight-rope walking has its danger, sword swallowing, cliff diving, fire fighting, auto racing, all these accredited lacerations do not compare to the available smash and dismemberment from the first-time heifer.

The problem is to attach machinery to the hallowed parts of a heifer without getting exterminated. Dairy farmers who are not consummate arbitrators, who never learn to gentle a cow with the stroke of their words go immediately extinct. Those who approach a cow with stainless steel suction without adequate preparation of a heifer's psyche are removed, usually feet first, from their profession.

I had heard tales of milkers kicked the full length of barn, of milkers, suction hose, surchingle, and stainless steel bucket propelled in level flight across the whole distance as well. I have heard of milkers kicked through windows. Milkers smashed flat. Milkers reduced to a puddle of blood and guts in the merest instant. All because the man or barn boy did not so fashion his words and his manner to settle the seething violence in a heifer. Here then the best theater of the agricult, a spell of literature and oratory so profound, so captivating the heifer forgot her original purpose and left her feet on the floor.

Every tit-puller knows when he was losing. A heifer's all-so-subtle shift to favor her better leg, or the wiggle of her nether side toe, perhaps a yellow glare in her eye, the twitch of her long violin-strung muscle. The dairyman's attention to the cocking of a heifer's intent is what saved many farmers their lives. This and that delicate, eternal parlay. Makes no difference if she is a one ton female, the man's hands are on her tits. One false move and she is going to kick his bucket. Seduction is the only recourse. Lucky for the world the practitioners of these skills are kept to their rural locations by the forces of twice-daily chores. Else daughters, wives and nieces everywhere would suffer the erosion of dairyman's words, words so smooth and so soothing as to build an economy on tits. And Lord Byron thought he was good.

Every farmboy knew the legends of great bovines brought to

honest work, and the supreme accolade, "tit-tamer." A title earned on the entry of the next heifer to the barn, a wild cow who has never been touched much less had vacuum attached.

My father said, and he said it 'cause he was a Republican, and 'cause he heard rumors about her, and 'cause every farmer probably thought as much, and it weren't meant for publication anyhow. My father said, and he didn't intend it meanly and only a little politically, and it had nothing to do with the war effort. My father said, actually he said all sorts of things in the confines of the barn that weren't meant for dissemination, meaning heard by females of any kind. My father said getting a heifer to take a milker took the same length of sweet elocution as to hang a milker on Mrs. Roosevelt during Democratic County Picnic. This without resort to the beer barrel.

Milking cows is an improbable vocation, the more you think about it the less likely it seems. I spent my life from the time I was knee high till released from the farm into the arms of matrimony in the service of tits. Thousands upon thousands of them. The principled and the unready, the wounded and unkind, the nervous, the suspicious and the resolved. I have talked, cajoled, implored, I have rubbed liniment, inserted tubes, picked scabs and sutured wounds. It was the second most dangerous art I ever practiced.

The Spring Assessment

T he spring assessment had the after-taste of one of Captain Quantrill's raids. The very same taint, a sourness in the back of the throat, a want for pitchfork revenge, a dull ache for murder in the first degree.

The host of the spring assessment and all the psychopathy as follows is the Town Assessor who according to statute is the only person under the advertisement of Lord God Geehova to have the right of full and indiscriminate trespass. Not even the Sheriff might come to a ploughman's cot and croft without a warrant, neither the Attorney General, John Wayne, or the Strategic Air Command. None except the Town Assessor has the right to prowl a man's keep and make value of it for which the household is taxed according to mill-rate of the municipality. A most vile tax, administered in a most vile way, all at the glean and eye of one man. A person who by the uncommon forfeits of nature is deprived of decency. Whose disregard of values was to invite accidental mutilation.

Assessors are in the corollaries of taxation, born without nerves. Their task requires a coolness in the glare of battle like none since the Somme. A willingness to die without utterance, cry, or oratory. Their cause is the assessment role and the tax on milk cows, saw logs, and improvements.

Assessors are chiefly known by their foul habits. Take the instance of a farmer from any common sampling, a good farmer, churched and hard-working, honest to a fault. A farmer who happened to build a pig shed, a simple shed, costing fifteen dollars for the nails and the hinges. All else of it born by that farm method known also to carrion birds. The boards second-hand, and as likely third. The galvanized roofing was also used, you can tell because the nail holes don't align with the framing and it is very evidently patched-over sheet tin. This obvious practice the assessor doesn't witness. Instead, according to his diagram of the farmstead, a new building has been added. New meaning it wasn't there last year. Accordingly he gives it value, modest by his thinking, and true enough to what it'd cost anyone else, say five hundred dollars. The assessor you see does not nor is he employed by the town board to know farmers and get to the root of farmers. The assessor is there to assign fair value. That is how the book says it, in reality he is there to tax. The farmer, as long as he has been a farmer, is a professional moocher and knows if this shed was of five hundred dollars made, he'd be this afternoon in Rio de Janeiro with the rest of the New Rich. Ladies and Gentlemen, what we have then is a contest in the guise of the ordinary.

Farmers since ancient times have contrived to obscure true value as caught in the gaze of the assessor. There is nothing illegal about this. The taxes are dutifully paid, if not necessarily according to the first calculations of the assessor.

New England farm architecture is the direct descendent of farmers fending off assessors. Historians will recount how this extended architecture was the result of winter, or state it was for convenience; it was not. A hen house was added to the woodshed, attached to the summer kitchen, the result connected to the lambing pen just beyond. In order followed the tractor shed, the farm shop with stove and calendar, and finally the barn at the end of this serpent. All one mutated vertebrae in a complex, interwoven jumble. Wasn't done for architecture but to confuse the assessor. To confuse, disorient and bring on stomach upset. Especially if the opinions of these buildings were not uniform. At this point no assessor can tell whether it is new shed or not.

Another tactic is to avoid paint. At all costs, avoid paint. Assessors value paint. You can tell right off when the hippy farmers move into the old farm buildings. They spread swings all over. They tame weeds. They buy paint. They do not understand the spring assessment. Assessors see paint as a manifestation of newness. Newness has implications of wealth, which is taxable.

The final and best defense against the assessor is the dog. No ordinary dog. Needed is a spring assessment dog. A dog the farmer is wise to import and pay for at the weekly rate. A mongrel cross-eyed dog, somewhere between a black lab dog and a tyrannojackalrex dog. A dog with a logging chain for a leash. A dog to inspire every bladder as ever sees it. A dog to give the assessor the idea they might just conduct the spring assessment from inside the car, with the windows rolled up, even if they steamed up some from his breath coming fast.

The spring assessment is nice. It is also mannerly. Lynching the Town Assessor is not. Every method short of that is fair.

There are other diversions, such as man-eating chickens, less actual man-eating as man-confounding. Chickens can be trained to undo shoelaces. Truly they exist, farmyards full of shoelace-devouring chickens. Animals capable of defending the farm against invasions of assessors, raving evangelists, gear-oil salesmen, welding rod suitors, and door-to-door statisticians.

Another method is to leave off spring cleaning of the loafing barn. Saving the calf pens and the chicken coops until the very week the assessor took circumnavigation of the town. It is charitable of the Legislature to tax by the calendar, values according to April 1st. We knew when the assessor was coming.

For the week or two around April 1st the more a farmer did to leave his settlement uninhabitable, the better off he was likely to be. Meaning volumes of manure, volumes of volatile aromatics as to make a practiced eyeball sweat, much less the assessor who is unaccustomed to explosive smells. Smells able to ruin supper and the company of a pair of wool trousers for a month after.

It is also to your advantage to let the milk cows out in the yard when word comes the assessor is headed down the road. No assessor worth his salt is likely to ask the number of cows from the practitioner, not without at least trying to count them himself. Being pinned twice against the barn fence by a friendly bunch of cows an assessor is more prone to take the herdsman's word on the count and be grateful. Anyway, assessors have a gaze that spoils criminality in farmers. A low-level Lord-God-Geehova-look like Moses used on the Red Sea and a farmer forgets about subtracting three titters and hard-milkers as shouldn't count anyway and neither those with hardware or who haven't delivered anything but a bull calf in four straight tries.

The spring assessment had a mood once and maybe still has. A spring like as not over-done with mud, mud in the whole township, not a stable inch of dry within a hundred miles and the assessor coming 'round. A farmer must defend his ground by whatever allies he can muster.

Farmcats

F armcats are less cats than Bengal tigers in a more conve-
nient form, cats best known by their fossil forms in saber
tooth, cats with paws the size of logarithms that lived in leg-
endary places like barns and granaries and woodsheds. They were
sly cats as all cats are, quick, rapid, velocited cats. But more they
were glacial cats that walked abroad at twenty-seven below,
prowlers in the night when mouse breath was visible above the
snow and hence grew fat cats.

Farmcats were the product of two mutually exclusive theorems.
One is an impulse to survive without equal in any other subject in
the animal kingdom and an opposite equal compulsion toward personal injury. These two opposite, mutually exclusive forces met
exactly at farmcat.

The basic reason for this is a cat, more than any other living
creature, pleasures in sleep. While others live to eat, like cows; to
fly, like pigeons; or like catholic animals, to multiply; the cat has
no greater meaning for existence than to luxuriate in undisturbed,
unencumbered sleep. No other animal has a torso so conducive to
sleep. Whether a rock, a tree limb, a bramble bush, a railroad tie, a
cat will make of it a bed. Hard surface, lumpy, bumpy, or plain
will a cat nap and wink away the day. No other animal is so born,

so gravitated to sleep, none so luxurious about it. Be it window ledge, rotten stump or chimney corner, there in due time a cat shall sleep. No instrument is necessary, loose a cat and in the space of a quarter hour this untutored student will have found the warmest place within reach and is there already asleep.

Among farmcats this instinct proves at once a serious flaw and a modest means of population control, for the warmest spot in the barn is nowhere more abundant or more luxuriant than in the straw, where till just a moment before the cow has lain. Warm cow-tempered straw. Cozy. Sleep inducing. Fat warmth of a kind rare to nature. Here can a cat troubled with all sorts of economic woes, business failures, family disputes, nervous disorders, stomach complaints sleep the sleep of the unfettered. Full PanaVision dream sleep of which there is no better and why cats have so many admirers.

A fool can tell you cow straw is no place to sleep because it is dangerous, particularly if you are smaller than the cow which a cat ordinarily is. This admonition stops other animals from pursuing sleep lust but not cats who believe in their one saving ability, that being born cats they are also velocitous beings that can wait until the last instant on the Day of Judgement to engage repentance, and still assure themselves eternity. Yet to the last second enjoy the comforts of heathen practice.

Alas, the only thing faster than a cat at repentance, and a cat is lightning at repentance, the only thing faster, as you've already guessed, is the cow taking back the warm spot. Farmcats live under the false impression the speed of a cow lying down is relative to the speed of a cow getting up. Cats don't appreciate tonnage going uphill is another animal from the same tonnage aimed downhill. A cow ain't rapid at nothing in the world with the exception of regaining the warm spot at which a quarter mile length of lightning and a black and white holstein have equal elapsed times.

Ordinarily a cat, farm or otherwise, can not get entirely killed by locomotion alone. Usually it takes a corresponding ingredient

to kill a cat, sadly this is the case with a cow coming in for a landing. No simple head on collision train wreck can kill a cat. This a
cat survives owing there is tangle to wreckage. A tangled wreck is
easy to survive if you are smaller than the average tangle. The reason people die in collisions that can not kill a cat is people are
more equal to the ratio of the wreckage. They get hammered,
chewed and torn off where a cat glides through same as small children, celibate priests, snakes, and convicted felons.

Problem with a cow lying down is the reduced size of tangle, a
horsefly might survive but a cat can't.

Wise farmcats learn early if they are any the bit observant that
the warmest place in the barn isn't the best choice. That others
continue to get snuffed out suggests wise cats are selfish about
their observations. Also that the second warmest spot in the barn
is rarer than the first. In most cases this is the electric motor driving the vacuum pump. It is here at the vacuum pump the twin
theorems of farmcats meet. The one will to live without equal; the
other to risk all manner of personal injury to do so.

An electric motor is for reasons of resistance a warm place,
offering penitent, even heat, the very best effort of modern technology. Every cat knows this. As the sunlit window ledge, the
warm rock, and the cabin hearth served a hundred generations of
cats before, the electric motor offered to cats, sovereign farmcats,
the haute couture of comfort. Soft messaging heat, the jacuzzi of
catdom, luxury beyond purrs to express. Those who know barns,
farmcats and vacuum pumps have guessed already the furtherance
of this tale. Alas the cat did not, or else is too seduced and com-
forted by electric heat to care.

A motor is connected to the vacuum pump via a vee-belt, in
itself no problem. The tragedy is the cat has a tail, a tail without
memory, wit, mindfulness or common sense. The cat as many
observers note is really two animals; one is the cat proper, the
other is the tail. They dwell together but are not otherwise related.

Notice the behavior of a cat gone a-hunting and finding the

succulent mouse. At the moment requiring total concentration and motionlessness, the cat poised and ready, except that damn tail. Flipping around gay as a kite, lolliegagging, playing jump rope with itself. The tail is a vegetarian and in confederacy with the mouse. That mouses do not die according to script is because they are forewarned by the tail, a moral tail if there ever was one.

Electric motors coupled to vee-belts love fingers, shirt sleeves, pant cuffs, whiskers, thumbs, noses, anything that protrudes. Nothing is more relished than a tail, an unthinking twitch is enough to satisfy the motor. The result is a sawed-off cat, on appearance alone convincing and lethal as a sawed-off shotgun. Here then the true identity and origin of the farmcat, like the farmer himself nipped of offending appendages and organs of low intelligence, though none of the amputations are voluntary the intellect of the remains is improved.

A cat is not an honest farmcat until it has begun the terrible duty of whittling itself down to size. The tail is sheer suburban excess, the tail is the biological equivalent of a Volvo, it is style and Swedish chrome plate, neither is a benefit to survival.

A true farmcat will go forth to improve itself. During the winter it gives up the tail, with spring a foot and foreleg are lost to the hay mower, soon after an eye to a squabble with a crow concerning dining rights on a roadkill. The cat's intelligence surging as each one of these life-threatening body parts is eradicated.

I have seen farmcats so rare and purified they were reduced to two legs, no tail, one glaring incandescent eye and most of the hair absent from its hide. So shorn of bad habits and regrettable impulses this cat is nearly immortal, it takes a direct hit from a meteorite to kill this residual kind of cat.

Wise farmers never fix their cats. To do so results in their complete immortality with nothing left to lure a cat into life-threatening behavior. The same is probably true of other animate types.

Toothpicks

O ut in the townships, out beyond the trailer parks, out past the perimeter of billboards, out where streets become roads. Out there in the wastes of the agricult exists a singular mark of education. Not education exactly, something closer to lineage, yet not that exactly either, tighter I think it is to prowess.

Most schoolchildren know Cyrus Noble invented the toothpick, what led Cyrus to the invention was his wright shop using only premium grade birch spokes. He wasn't interested in oak 'cause oak gave a hard ride. Cyrus could tell in ten rods whether a wagon or surrey were hung on oak spokes, whether maple, or the more luxuriant ride of birch. Cyrus called them spooks.

What turned Cyrus to birch in the first place was the lack of oak in his own woods, and he set about fixing birch up as a religion seeing as oak were avoiding him. Cyrus said oak were an endangered resource if folks kept using oak for spooks like there were no tomorrow and according to his calculations all the oak would be gone from the North Yankee continent by the middle of the twentieth century. Didn't personally matter to him 'cause he had birch. Cyrus ever the entrepreneur set up a chair business for his dim-witted cousin Oscar Sorghum owing Oscar could make a chair with plumb legs on the first try. Any carpenter knows this is prodigious, making a chair as sits plumb the first time. Darn miraculous besides what with Oscar being no more natural than a set screw.

Everything in the birch spook business was going fine till Rudolph Diesel and Gottlieb Daimler collided with history. Cyrus always thought automobiles had been a heck more attractive left with spook wheels instead of stomped tin.

Cyrus Noble's Birch Spook Corporation was in shambles, Cyrus feeling plain useless, his only real ambition to go drown himself in Bromfield's creek but the water was low so he couldn't gain any honor there either. In the midst of this depression he messed about in the vacant spook works and in a fit of meanness let the lathe spin a blank using the far inside to far outside gang pulleys propelling the birch in the neighborhood of an extravagant dizzy. Birch blanks weren't intended to endure such, at which point lignum isn't a satisfactory glue and the blank burst into a zillion pieces, all of them evenly sized.

Cyrus were cleaning up the floor when he used one of the pokes to pry out a popcorn hull from the night before. Hmm, you don't suppose?

Within a week Cyrus had geared up a national campaign endorsing his patent birch toothpicks. Sam Clemens and Teddy Roosevelt were lined up as proponents, Cyrus having switched them over from kitchen matches. Clemens despite his agreement to join the ministry had to go die 'cause his comet came back and it being his only ride to high ground or risk a detour.

Before the age of the toothbrush, before the onslaught of pastes, gums, tooth powders, soda washes, and minty gels, the act of oral hygiene stood at a pretty low state. Kissing a person's mouth was second best, after kissing a gangrenous wound. The only defense favoring of one mouth touching another being Cyrus

Noble's birch picks.

Modern toothpick connoisseurs are divided on the issue of flats or rounds, this a reference to the shape. There are flat societies and round societies in the rural parts whose existence gains a queer look from village folk. My father preferred flats. Flats are just right with false teeth when the user wants a loitering sort of pick. But if it's a pry bar you're after, round is what you want. A flat toothpick allows fancy maneuvers though it tires rapidly, while a round one lasts all morning. If aggravation you got, round is what you want. With toothpicks the science of psychology can be avoided, schizophrenics can set one personality to chewing the toothpick while the clearer-headed of the two steers. Homicidal maniacs can't perform with a toothpick in their yap, neither can adulterers; the toothpick is one of the most devoted self-improving appliances ever invented by man, every unpleasant trait postponed if not moderated.

Psychologists who take their residency at a feedmill know good mental health begins with a toothpick. Unfortunately since practitioners do not take their clinical residency at feedmills there is a shortage of psychologists recommending toothpicks to the stressed-out.

Long long ago, a pioneering behaviorist observed that gnawing animals, i.e. beavers, Norwegians, rabbits, moose, camels, horses, chipmunks, and woodpecks refused to demonstrate any evidence of anxiety-driven illness. They did not fidget, weren't prone to complaint and could ignore teenagers without going, as the phrase has it, crazy. They entirely avoided symptomatic depression, saved from mental distress by gnawing on a companionable length of stick with no aftertaste and a minimum of slivers.

Sadly this early observer of mental health was run over by a truck and his remarkable discovery died with him and Sigmund Freud took over, the rest as they say is a subject for another session. Freud did to mental disease what William Shakespeare did to English Lit, he gave it a professional standing, same what Moses did for lawyers five thousand years before, precluding every Tom, Dick and Harry from practicing law. The same is true for literature and psychiatry, a circumstance that continues to this very day.

An accomplished toothpick artist never has to touch the thing with his hands but can work it back and forth using muscles that otherwise could be talking. Despite observations to the contrary talk hasn't improved the human condition, needed is a prosthesis for talk, this where toothpicks come in. A person raised to toothpicks don't need cigarettes, chew, cigars, pipes, gumballs, chewing resins, suckers, lollipops, lozenges, mints, or chocolates. Don't need prayer, confession, mantras, hymns, swear words or know which way is east, 'cept maybe as the finish coat.

The author does not understood why high class restaurants don't have humidors of select toothpicks to trot out with the Madeira. Some of the best versions of words ever heard by mankind were marinated with a toothpick. It may be jumping to conclusions but it seems toothpicks are connected to higher brain function.

It is hard to say enough about toothpicks, they look dashing on a person, especially fine with a tuxedo shirt and black tie. Whole afternoons slide away between two grown men at the fence, each tending a toothpick and only the incidental word. You can't very well point out what is misguided, malcontent, onerous or otherwise mucked up on another person when there's a clinical objective to chew on.

Opinion is the worst sin a person can commit. Stealing, adultery, murder are the result of opinion. Halt opinion and human betterment is assured. A practitioner of the opinion professions who has not equipped their affliction with a toothpick is a danger to society. Politics, the ministry, journalism require the toothpick, agriculture is suicidal without its council. No quicker way is there to improve the human condition than to gnaw on something that can't bite back.

Dirt Roads

I used to think righteousness came in blacktop. I thought this way because the townroad by our place wasn't righteous, meaning it was dirt and had been dirt and sometimes less than dirt since the Great Ice.

I wondered about roads when I was a kid. Kids think about roads. Like why a road is in one place and not another. Or how a road got a crook in it on account a big elm once stood in the way and ever after the crook stood, even though the elm was gone, which is a long shadow. Or how once a road is born it hardly ever dies. It is the business of commerce to build roads but nothing has the equal charge to unbuild them. Doesn't seem fair somehow; a force should exist equal to roads, to undo them sure as do them. Though everybody knows there ain't no such force, an anti-road force.

The road by our place was dirt, it started at Dunnegan's barn on the stage road and struck off south for Plainfield with the length of the marsh and Mosquito Bluff in between. One long stretch of dirt except for the elm planks on the bridges. The map showed the road as straight; it wasn't. Funny how it wasn't, the land is sure flat enough with fewer lumps than Mama's oatmeal. The road wasn't plumb at all, instead sashayed and quibbled, canted this way, tilted that, more a sailing ship heeling at a breeze.

The road had a kind of animation in it you wouldn't expect from a road, least not a dirt road going pretty much of nowhere, as if the road was trying to conceal where it was going. This kept some folks from trying.

The dirt road had a happiness I didn't appreciate until much later. Neither did I understand that dirt provided some measure of defense, it held back the riff-raff and asparagus thieves 'cause a dirt road looks a heck more unreliable than blacktop. This the reason a farmer keeps a dog of mixed parentage—a dirt road kinda bristles and shows its teeth and folks who took this as strange went by another length of road.

A dirt road was like having a moat around the township, a castle wall with arrow slits and draw bridges and battlements. We had relatives who never visited in the summer knowing our road was dirt because they didn't want to blemish their car. Dust they couldn't roll the windows tight enough to keep out of the car, a warm day about killed them if they tried to visit. Folks who feel this way about their cars aren't worth socializing with. People who defend polish on cars ain't got anything interesting to say 'cause polish matters so darn much they'll bore you to death about their trip to Florida or Yellowstone but never once were they to Mosquito Bluff 'cause the road is dirt and Mosquito Bluff don't have a brochure or a window sticker.

Let it rain and a dirt road is even more protection. Nobody went by. Not even trout killers who knew about trout thick as maggots under Eckel's Bridge.

A dirt road had character. In the hollow the road was a mood different than at the rise. A person walking the road knew the moods, in one place given to sandburrs and gravel, in another bouncing bet and marigolds. On a dirt road you weren't ever surprised by cars, the road had 'em spotted long before and the prop-wash of stones and sand clattered after in an unorchestrated way.

A kid who lived on a dirt road got home by the time his old

man said 'cause he couldn't sneak in like the kid who lived on blacktop who'd cut the ignition two hundred yards off and coast home silent as a well-fed owl. On dirt a car don't coast and the gravel under the tires goes off like firecrackers.

I learned to drag race on dirt roads. Drop the clutch on a Hyper-dyne DeSoto with red wheels and she just sat there, digging like a badger, three inches down already. It was awhile before kids bred and raised on dirt roads realized this wasn't the original intent. We thought the term was dug race and it made sense on a dirt road until a village kid suggested we do it on blacktop. He must have wondered why we looked at him peculiar. You can't dug race on blacktop for criminies sake. All as'll happen is to rub your tires off in black sorta marks. We eventually realized this was the result desired. A dirt road had a heck more spectacle to offer.

The townroad never had a speed limit. Didn't need to, dirt took care of that. At thirty-eight miles an hour a car picked up a contrail including a resident swarm of gravel. At forty-five the little swarm became more a plague, most of it about windshield height. The faster the car went the longer the gravel hung in midair, the effect is about equal to discharging a load of buckshot at a passing car.

On dirt the speed limit wasn't as much governed by the legisla-ture as by the road itself. Turtles used the road to incubate their eggs, killdeer nested at the edge but the dirt road never did favor the bicycle.

I have yet, though long past a kid, certain untamed affections for dirt roads. A quarter mile west the townroad turns dirt. Some hold this is an unimproved and backward condition and annually petition the town men to blacktop this heathen attitude.

I like dirt roads because they slow me down, put a little drag on the line of progress. After a couple rainy days in a row a dirt road will separate out a cubic volume of farm country like nothing else short of atomic war. The place gets to be alone for awhile. Time dawdles. Nothing short of a tractor trusts a townroad in a mood like this.

People tell me I'm not up on my issues. How the spotted owl is in trouble and the loon and old growth redwoods. They giggle when I tell them about protecting the dirt road between here and Bancroft, how it holds a pose on a marsh evening, faithful to something I can't quite grasp. Some shaping force, some keeping manner, all in the guise of a dirt road.

Two Kinds of
Farm Dogs

People who think they know something about country probably don't know about farm dogs. There is more than one kind of farm dog, honest fact there be two kinds; the country is better off for this misunderstanding.

The standard farm dog is the one of universal appellation. This the definitive country dog widely perceived as useful to agriculture, it chases cows and herds sheep, sometimes in the desired direction. More advanced forms of this animal have been successfully trained to mend fence and drive tractors. As a result they are allowed the accommodations of their choice; either to dwell under the porch or take refuge behind the kitchen stove. A better situation than accorded the rest of the semi-domestic animals dwelling in the farmhouse.

The lesser known farm dog does not do anything modern, meaning it is not liability conscious. There are farmers who think this is useful. This dog is your basic revenge unit dating back to evil times when victorious Christians turned ancestors of the same loose on the battlefield to minister to the wounded and dying, and versions of it have been enlisted to fulfill the last desperate measure of home protection. Since farmers generally don't own anything worth stealing, the deployment of this dog on the farmstead is frivolous, in fact more entertainment than defense.

In the farmtowns the secret purpose of this dog was birth control, practiced on any farmkid so foolish to venture the road inhabited by his majesty, the antediluvian ditch dog. Because of the ditch dog, there were woods never visited, creeks never fished, deserted homes never investigated; the ditch dog or its rumor stood in the way. A dog, so legend had it, capable of ingesting not only the kid but chewing up and swallowing the bicycle. From the car window we'd spy the remains of disemboweled bikes laying in the ditch, or a stray article of clothing; all that remained of the careless kid.

Ditch dogs had one goal in life, to eat any kid caught going past and digest them at their considerable leisure among the lilacs. Their owners did not require the augmentation of radio and television for their evening's entertainment. I believe they purposely dug the finest of irrigation pits resulting in the best possible swimming hole in the solar system, and nurtured vast groves of succulent blackberries, all to entice neighborhood kids. And watch the ensuing spectacle from their front porch. As entertaining were asparagus pickers, equally lured, who ambled by only to be set after by the ditch dog. The Christians and the lions weren't half so theatrical.

It is a known fact there were farmers who imported the finest Tibetan asparagus for the express purpose of seeding down the length of their road. Was bait. A mischievous and cruel bait. Because they were too cheap to buy a television. There is nothing more antic than an asparagus picker pursued by a long-legged artillery shell. The remains of the victim fertilized an ever-lusher stand of that sinister grass.

The best swimming hole this side of Mars was sometimes too blamed intoxicating to ignore, hence our only option was to risk the ditch dog, the sling-shot the standard counter-measure. Problem being the sling-shot is a two-hand device, meaning you had to get off the bike to use it and if you missed you were lilacs.

The BB gun was altogether nother. A kid felt some degree of
safety with a BB gun in a gunny sack. Unfortunately Daisys and
Crosmans didn't come semi-auto. Doing a lever-action Red Ryder
at speed, on a bicycle, on a ditch dog road, was dangerous. If the
dog didn't get you, the bicycle did.

I knew farmkids who ventured a ditch dog road in small, tense
swarms. Armed with BB guns and intent on a naked swim. Guns
cocked. Pedaling as slow as a dirt road allows. Daring the dog to
emerge from the lilacs. High Noon. On ditch dog road.

Some old instinct stirred in the ditch dog's brain, his sulfurous
eyes mellowed to the color of johnny cake. It yawned. It didn't feel
like chasing bicycles. The folks on the front porch thought better
of television. For the first time in a thousand years a living kid
passed that farmhouse beneath the gaze of a ditch dog whose sad
eyes watched the bicycle cavalry chime by. It was almost ...
maudlin. Sure, the ditch dog still sic after asparagus pickers but
doubt had entered its mind. A dog with a conscience is no longer a
real ditch dog. Now it tested the breeze for the hint of sewing
machine oil known to super-charge BB guns.

As a species, ditch dogs have pretty well died out, mostly due
to blacktop. On a dirt road a ditch dog can hear the scrunch of
gravel beneath a bicycle tire a half mile off. He can prepare his
attack. Prewarm his juices. A dirt road was exactly like that long
panoramic view above the Serengeti Plain. Like it or not, you
knew one of the wildebeest was gonna end up somebody's supper.
Ditch dog ecology is the same.

It is probably too late to wonder what dirt roads and the cultivation of ditch dogs might have done for urban sprawl. Maybe
there be creeks out there Trout Unlimited wouldn't yet know
about, and lilacs line every road with lush asparagus in between.
Farmkids now have other fates open to them; they can become
bankers and lawyers and English professors because the balance
of nature is tilted. Because paved roads and BB guns ended the
long reign of ditch dogs.

Riding the Fair

Going to the fair was once the only release from summer chores, this what fairs have always meant to rustic people. Fairs are exotic isles of colorful tents, prized animals bathed and combed to Eden-like perfection. Fairs are sawdust, beer tents, games of chance Warren Spahn couldn't win, pastel bears, flickering lights, cotton candy, and corn stalks that can't stand erect in the exhibit building.

To a kid fairs are scary and disorienting, all the people, all the smells mixed together, from the cattle barn to the hot dog stand. The tangled noise of barkers, cries of delight and terror, the lowing of cows and wail of a lost child. The fair is a medieval abduction, its nebulous glow and panjandrum calls, the weird food and burlesque thrills a little left of household sin.

Like all country people we went to every fair in driving distance, the announcement "going to the fair" given on a Sunday morning abrogated the requirement of church attendance. The morning hour spent driving to Wausau or Weywauwega or the Marshfield. Once every self-respecting community had a fair. Since the time of Arthur it has been so, the tents and pick-pockets, the jousts and demolition derbies, beer tents, polka bands, and cut-off shorts, eggplant and canned beans, immaculate rows, potatoes,

squash and kohlrabi combined with the squeals from victims on
the Ferris wheel.

Eventually we went to the fairs by ourselves, farmboys in a
pickup truck with t-shirt sleeves rolled over blocks of wood to
look like a pack of cigarettes. The truck had been hosed out, the
scattered tools and fencewire removed, the oats vacuumed from
the corners of the cab and the crevice of the seat. We hung a pair
of dice from the mirror, oiled the tires and were ready for the fair.

I was chiefly interested in the fragrant girls in gossamer
blouses that strolled the midway in self-protecting bunches throwing teasing looks over their white shoulders. An enormous pimple
always seemed to nest in the space between my eyes at fair time. A
pimple so vivid I resembled a gunshot victim, lacking only the
powder burns of authenticity. The chance of girls wasn't good.

The object of the fair thence became to tame every thrill ride,
and in a manner bordering on suicide, so heckle the operator that
he might unleash his machine on us. It was a known fact in those
days that many fair rides had a safe operating speed, and another
more interesting velocity when the governor was wedged open. A
carni man sufficiently badgered attempted to empty your stomach
utilizing the full thirty foot diameter of a tilt-a-whirl, at twice the
normal speed.

They'd do this when the crowd thinned out or the rain came
and the only thing left at the fair were farmboys, some of them
gunshot between the eyes and a too-angular block of wood rolled
in their sleeves.

Once we had to beg the guy to let us off, after forty minutes at
a speed that did credit to astronaut training we were famished for
solid ground. The block of wood had been thrown at the operator
only to miss badly and censure any chance of diplomacy for
another full ten minutes. When he finally stopped we stumbled off
only to fall to the sawdust earth amid the half licked suckers, puddles, spit, vomit, and sodden popcorn. His laughter burning our

pickup truck souls.

Vomit was the ultimate indicator of a great fair ride. The rides always occupied the same spot year after year and over time a kind of organic plebiscite accumulated, electing the best ride. Vomit deposited over the years resembles blacktop, the same chewed and recycled look, the crust blackened over time.

A real maelstrom of a ride acquired a pavement surrounding its spot on the fair grounds. You could feel it underfoot as you approached the ride if you wore soft shoes. We always wore Keds to the fair so it was usually the guys in motorcycle boots and high-tops who barfed 'cause they had no sense of the innate energy in a ride. They couldn't feel the ground harden under the sawdust and they had already consumed three orange pops, two corn dogs, and had just started a wad of Cow-Muzzle brand bubble gum that smells of internal organs and stomach acid. Which you don't really comprehend until you're on the ride, spinning dizzily and then that bubble gum smell overwhelms. I believe they only sold Cow-Muzzle brand bubble gum at fairs.

My brother went to the State Fair once and returned home pallorous from the roller coaster. They took the thing down before I had a chance to ride the same and see whether I could keep my stomach.

Probably the best fair ride ever consisted of two cone-shaped capsules attached to revolving arms that whirred in one direction while the cages revolved on another axis entirely. If you could hold your stomach on "The Bullet" you could hold it anywhere. The ground beneath the Bullet was firm as a dance floor and it was not wise to stand in spilling distance of that instrument of torture.

After awhile a semi-professional sensibility develops and you readily knew a good ride from a mediocre ride. We'd hang around the good ones driven by the sadistic tattooed operator with alligator teeth. Eyeing other farmboys with blocks of wood rolled in their sleeves, daring them with our glances, the Betcha-Puke look. We knew of the levers that subjected the cages to violence only an atom smasher knew. We'd mutter insults at the executioner, to wipe the earth with them, and he'd try his devil best to wring their innards out. They as a mutual favor heckled for us so we felt our stomachs nestled next to our tonsils, sweat beading on our foreheads, our knuckles white as a porch post.

We emerged trying to look cheerful, unaffected, our toothy grin an attempt to hold in our displaced organs. God help us if anyone nearby was chewing Cow-Muzzle bubble gum. We leaned heavily on the fence, in truth wanting to lie down, swallowing far more often than is necessary. Offering only a feeble jeer as another set of late-night riders boarded the horror.

In the end we drove home penitent as the moon. The windows of the truck open, our elbows out, we felt mutilated and spent. And it was exactly wonderful.

Why Farmers Golf

For reasons of moral purity I do not golf. Other than that, I have no particular reason not to, golf seems harmless enough. But when I think about it, this again is reason enough not to golf.

I have friends, neighbors and kinsmen who golf, many of whom are farmers, so I am curious why farmers golf.

Straight away anyone can see the sport of golf is awful cruel to a little bittie ball, which is not only abused but apparently suffers a skin ailment. I have a sneaking suspicion golf is not what it appears on the surface to represent, instead is some kind of Freudian therapy where mature persons use a wicked length of stick to strike back at the psychological forces oppressing them. The type of mean streak once reserved for hand to hand combat.

My concerns about golf are the connection of golf to an earlier Scottish custom and knowing most things the Scots do relates to their position as the most war-like race in human history. The world well knows these are the people who single-handedly invented whisky, temperance, sword play, armistice, tartan weave, men in skirts, oats unfit for horses, bagpipes, which are less music than vented stomach complaint, monsters in puddles, ghosts in castles, stone pickin' as sport, and in a last desperate attempt at profundity, the game of golf.

Golf started in a pasture, in particular a sheep pasture where shepherds with not enough to occupy their minds took to whacking at stones with their walking sticks. A sport to relieve the awful boredom attendant to watching sheep, where either a shepherd gets involved with religion—as amply documented by history—or else commences to look at sheep in a romantic context. The Scots found neither prospect very commendable, this where golf intervened.

As we know, all sports are therapeutic. Sport is without doubt the most appropriate intercession, where the anger at whatever is chasing you can be expressed in a harmless way. Sport is the one vital alternative to murder, politics, agriculture, marriage, business, warfare, and education. Golf is how civilization attempts to disarm otherwise nasty mental attitudes. The Scottish predecessors understood this on account they were terrible prone to warfare themselves and the only thing between them and total annihilation was emotional displacement, in other words learning to beat up an innocent white ball. The symbolism plain to see, the little white thing is their soul and the stick is the means of ethical enlightenment.

That golf came to exist at the same time sheep agriculture went in decline is no mere accident. Sheep and golf require the same basic resource, short grass. This because sheep can't eat except hunched over and little balls get lost in tall grass. Open space is also necessary because both sheep and golfers smell. Actually golf doesn't smell as much as the open space is the best habitat for swearing. If participants in basketball, baseball, hockey or tennis said what a golfer said, they'd be thrown in the showers so fast their shoelaces would burn. Golf was so designed by ancestral Scots as a remedy for humanity's stifled verbal expression. Baseball evolved around stealing and chewing tobacco, football followed the customs of beheading and bell-ringing, basketball developed around the need to wear colored underwear and jump. Only golf single-mindedly attached itself to literary relief.

Yet why farmers should golf is open to question. Farmers have fields to swear in and tractor noise sufficient to disguise foul language, and thus far the DNR has not put limits on this discharge. It doesn't require much research to note what is lacking in agriculture is the behavioral violence golf allows and normal tractor piloting does not. I did say normal tractor operation. Add to this one more innovation of golf, cheating.

Ordinarily the arithmetic involved for counting strokes ought not present any difficulty to educated persons; surprisingly it does. People who can otherwise tell the difference between one wife and two, fifty miles an hour and seventy, two scoops of ice cream and three, two eggs or three, can not understand the difference between four strokes and five. People who remember the name of the third cousin of their great grandfather twice removed can not exactly recall whether it was six strokes at the third hole or three strokes at the sixth. Being frugal as the Scots intended, they put down three.

Despite these enumerated causations for golf, they still do not provide any reason why those in agriculture can gain benefit from it. There is a reason and a good one. A farmer who golfs will not threaten his best chance at a profit by surplus work. I realize this sounds confusing to those accustomed to other occupations. The central thesis is the more farmers golf, the less they are likely to over-do what the field has in mind. Golf is a better modifier of agricultural sin than drought, floods, and hailstorms combined. Never mind the unsettling predictions of bovine growth hormone, so long as farmers are inoculated once or twice a week with a need to swing a stick at an innocent but diseased ball prices will maintain themselves just fine.

Were I the Secretary of Argueculture I would not delve into set-asides, soil banks, wetland protection, buy-outs, feed grains, foreign markets or diversified production. Instead I'd provide every farmer and his apprentice with a set of golf clubs and limousine to a nearby golf course at least twice a week from April to

November. Not only would the man's psychological health improve but so too his economy. To insure the result I'd build a golf course in every township for farmers only and if they didn't show up I'd shoot 'em for uncapitalistic activities and because they're too damn stupid to chance their procreating.

At the outset I admitted I didn't golf because I recognized it for the useless business it is; I now realize golf is more effective than any government program, besides being a genuine inspiration to ritual violence and verbal expression. I intend to mend my ways now that I have seen the light.

'Tis an Old
Scots Tradition

S ome races attract bad habits more often than others, some
are highly selective in their choice of garrybaggie gauds.
The Scots have gatten away with both.

Among the hale-jing-bang of Scots frauds is the specialized
Scots compulsion toward lanely stane, rocks and other haired,
imponderable, granite objects. It is mare than bad habit this veritable Scots compulsion to admire stane.

Anywhere in the weirld the Scots have gatten themselves hame
they set up the most geen yochkie freet o' nothing so much as a
fack o' stane. So afrontary are they, their admiration o' stane might
be conflabed for congregate wearship of same said stane.

'Tis not da Scots wearship stane as are impressed by their
immovable nature. This exactlie the same sentiment attached to Gaud
the almighty who ain moved off his heft since da book of Genesis.

Everywhair in the weirld that Scots have gatten themselves lost
they take up their ancient auld habit of looking unto stane, if stane
are not available they import them for this pearpuss. Don't matt'r
if the far-flung reaches of earth have nay hedder, nay kilts, nay
lamb stew, nay even atemeal, which is a mare gross sort of sacrilege but even that d'na matt'r as long as they have stane and
immovabell stane to look after.

Ye will see this where e'r Scots folk ha'been, the stane they
have adored left after them, cairns, hobnobs, and monuments of
stane, granites an' marbles an' sanestane monoliths, stane bigger
than a wee mannie can by all that is right move, standing aboot the
countryside, this the certain mark of a Scot.

Ev'r since stanehedge and some before Scots been cobbling
stane and for nay mare reason than to luke at the humble lesson o'
it, that ye air smeller than the stane. A mannie ken this, 'e kens the
most of it.

'Tis an auld Scots custom to admire stane, to build in their
hamelands cemeteries with stane bigger than the mannie was in
life, build stane walls and stane closes and stane keeps and only
the Scots will leave stane put jes' to admire it. Where e'er ye get in
the weirld ye'll find where Scots h've gone rune the big stane.
Other races might have deenimited stane, took leevers and ox to
set them elsewheres but no' the Scots. Wigh they'll even name the
stane and bear it flowers and talk unto it like stane be a parson
with sociable qualities.

Too Scots weel put stain is heetery sairkles and leave 'em to
puzzle the generations. Was the Scots who tout the Maya and
Aztecs every bit of their stane-pile gaud. An' Easter island was
sure enough populated by Scots as those enormousie stane have
the rouk look of Scots about them. An' the pyramids look very
seespishus of Scotfolk bein' in charge if maybe a leetle too refined
for a pure stane-kennin' Scots.

So when this day ends and ye have the bairns abeddie and the
hounds have quiet dune, sit by the fire kill and settle in your kilt and
deem an auld Scots custom contrived to put the imponderable at
everyhand. While a crude form of wearship it do keep the mannie
sort humble and that is the heal idee. So on January 25th a toast of
lammer wine to Bobbie Burns' birth and wee Scots souls everywhair.

Glossary

Atemeal—oatmeal

Conflabed—confused

Deenimite—dynamite

Fack—pile

Freet—fancy, whim

Garrybaggie—stomach of an unfledged bird

Gatten—gotten

Gaud—habit, prank, god, but not usually in the same breath

Gaukie—foolish

Geen yochkie—covetous, greedy

Haired—hard

Hale-jing-bang—whole thing, the entire shegosh

Hame—home

Hameland—homeland

Hedder—heather

Heetery—scary

Heft—pasture

Insight—tools kept indoors

Kill—fireside

Kilt—rolled up sleeves or pantlegs, a pant worn by males of prodigious sexual energy in order to keep their temperature remotely close to normal human beings

Ken—know, knows

Lammer wine—an amber wine famous in legend reputedly dandelion, esteemed as the elixir of immortality

Lanely—lonely

Luke—look

Mannie—mankind

Mare—more

Parson—person

Pearpuss—purpose

Rouk—disturbance, disturbed
Rune—round
Sairkles—circles
Smeller—smaller
Stainukenning—stoneknowing
Stane—stone
Tout—taught
Wearship—worship
Weirld—world, wold

Country Waving

Farmers have cause enough to visit psychiatrists, a cause equal to or better than average disenchantment. But farmers don't visit psychiatrists and not only because it costs more than an engine overhaul kit, rather farmers have a substitute. A therapy that provides a pretty fair assessment of the mental state and at a reasonable price, which can't be said for shrink-wrap.

When farmers pass on the road, they wave. How a neighbor waves adequately reveals his/her frame of mind and the condition of the subsoil as well. Hands tell it all, hands are honest organs.

The tongue is an altogether untrustworthy device. It dwells in a burrow, it's a slimy critter without a bone in its body, its vocation is noise, and often as not we don't know if the tongue is uttering the sound or the burrow is. At times even the teeth get involved, never trust biting machinery to say what is genuine.

Hands are honest. Hands are out in the open, they are used to exposure, hands can not avoid inspection. Hands are like a mug shot, no make-up, no soft focus, no blemish removal, every personal tick is evident. It doesn't take a therapy session or intravenous sodium Pentothal to know how your neighbor is doing, the hands, the wave on the road tell all.

Farmers know this. This is why farmers try to formalize the

wave to mask their state of mind, 'cause they don't want every darn fool to know their mood. Don't work though, 'cause hands are too blame honest.

My brother for instance, when we meet on the road he doesn't overtly wave...why should he, we're brothers? Still it doesn't seem right not to wave even if it looks silly. His wave consists of a raised index finger though the hand never lets go of the steering wheel. It is not much of a wave but from it I can tell my brother's mental state.

Like when only the knuckle moves. As you might guess, things aren't going good. At other times two or three fingers try to wave: for my brother this is ebullience, it's eight-dollar potatoes, a great night at the bowling alley, for him it's a veritable ecstasy. Means IRS bought the explanation of line 17 on Schedule Y we sent to them last month.

Country waving is chock full of etiquette. If for example you are passing the neighbor's place and notice they are busy reattaching a severed limb to the hired man, at this point a full-length wave is an intrusion because in country waving, a wave given must be acknowledged on pain of death. Same goes for the neighbor with both hands on a haybale or shingling the suicide slope on the barn roof. A full return wave with all the nuances and sub-paragraphs included is hazardous to the health of the second party.

To solve this farmers have learned not to wave but nod their head. It's acknowledgment but not a whole heck else. This is how farmers wave to strangers using their road on a Saturday morning to go fishing or worse, steal their asparagus. It consists of jutting out the jaw and waggling the lower end of the skull. Amish folks greet non-Amish folks like this all the time, it's hello enough for infidels. Same by the guy hanging shingles on the eighty-nine degree barn roof.

Not waving back at all is a sin. Neighborhood feuds have started because a neighbor didn't wave back. All farmers understand this diplomacy, screw one up and it could be nuclear war, neighborhood-style.

Which is why when passing the neighbor's place you must re-wave if they didn't see the first attempt. Like they were grabbing for the next rung and couldn't wave until they got latched on again. In the country it is important to wave until you get the thing done, even if it means backing up the tractor.

My cousin who farms down the road has a unique wave. His voice is no more elegant than a crow's but his wave is an act of sophistication and grace, the smoothest hand motion this side of a strip tease show.

I can't begin to tell you how good it feels inside to drive by his place and he perform that wave, I feel anointed. It makes my whole day, never mind my cousin and I can argue the opposite sides of any political or mineral spectrum till the cows come home, his wave heals everything.

My cousin waves the same as a minister I once knew gave his morning benediction. Whose raised hand over the congregation wasn't a limp banana but stretched out with the tendons exposed and the fingers soaring over us like an angel host. The congregation didn't ordinarily see this 'cause their heads were bowed. Being an eyes-open doubter I saw that hand, saw it lift out of the man's spirit and go with us to the barns and fields. Hands can do what a tree swallow wouldn't try.

Country waving is why I'm of a mind to burn out the squatters who dab their ticky-tacky houses on the country roads but teach at the university. Not one of them has ever learned to wave. They think unless they've met you formally they don't have to, that their hurry counts for more than anybody else's hurry. Besides, they're listening to Bach on the state station.

Country waving as I learned it says you're supposed to wave at everybody whether you know them or not. And there ain't a senti-ment more crippling than waving at someone and not getting a return echo. Same as swinging hard at a pitch and missing entire, hurts to smack up against that much emptiness. Like kissing an inflatable lady.

A neighbor hates my guts 'cause I raise potatoes and use pesticides and don't think highly of organic. Don't matter, when I meet her on the road I wave, admittedly a philosophically reserved wave. Think she waves back? No sir. She' running on village mores where they don't wave to enemies. According to country custom if you meet Adolf Hitler on the road you wave.

Waving is how you know it's a country road in the first place. Out here waving is sometimes the only thing we got that passes for a humanity between milking, weeding beans and hilling potatoes, a kind of last-ditch attempt at sanity. Waving is more country than twanging guitars, cowboy boots and John Deere rolled together. Waving at every living thing, including a few trees and a companionable field is how you know everything is OK.

Kicker

Wheee. Normally adults are banished from the word. *Wheee* coming from a person forty solar years or more has the same uncouth injury as an expletive from a young mouth. Surprising that something as mundane and repetitive as winter can extract from the hypnotic trance of the fossilized adult a sentiment like *Wheee!*

Whee is the sole prerogative of winter; summer, spring or fall can only practice a minor chord whee. If the reader does not believe it, the evidence can be gathered immediately. I shall poll the readership. How many of you have ever said *Wheee* to a winter day? Raise your hands. Now how many have ever said *Wheee* to a summer, spring or fall day? See? How's that for evidence? Admittedly the readership as meets at this pub every Wednesday evening is an eclectic and strange crew and probably not representative of the natural curve of political persuasion. Still, our poll indicates only one out of eight of you utter *Wheee* in a season other than winter.

We know why. A red-haired friend of mine was raised in the ornery emptiness of western Minnesota where winter evolved a prize strain of homo-erectus. My friend said of winter and *Wheee,* there were days known in Minniesorta as "— kickers." The dash indicates she typically precedes the verb form with a casual expletive apparently used by Minniesortas to express an inarticulate sensory overload. The reader will excuse the utterance as a casual folk-saying of an otherwise barbarous people. Insult is not intended, it is a standard expression of inbred Minniesortas, reflecting their innate relationship with winter and the *Wheee* quotient.

"A kicker," to render the term polite for print media, is a winter storm above and beyond the standard measure. A reference to weather beyond the routine margins of northern disposition. Recognize here that most of humanity, given the onset of twenty degree weather much less twenty below, have sufficient intelligence to vacate the premises. This is an advantage for the remaining primitives since it evacuates from the north those people not fitted by nature to accept meteorological cruelty. The result is more space for those perverse enough to stay. And as a special favor, northern winter attempts occasionally to kill off even the natives, this keeps everything indigenously honest. A winterer, or as the French-Canucks say, the *hivernaut* for hibernator, is then a specialized animal.

Northerners appreciate winter the same way a stock-car racing fan appreciates a good race; it is not a good race without a good wreck. The wreck of winter goes by the name previously mentioned, "kicker," with or without the expletive attached. To understand the specialized nerves of a Minniesorta or other northern hivernaut it is necessary to realize twenty below by itself is not close to a kicker. Not even forty below. Inconvenient and death to car batteries perhaps, but not anything spastically homicidal like a kicker. Mars, which has chilly weather, where carbon dioxide falls as snow, does not qualify as a kicker because a kicker is more than moderate insult. A kicker is closer to Indian war than it is mere inconvenience, more bodily harm than common hazard. A kicker is an attempt of the Darwinian Universe to balance human numbers by the simplest, most direct means possible. Hivernauts believe this is a conscious and premeditated policy to keep marimba bands from exceeding their normal range.

Northern folk can sense when a kicker is due. My red-haired friend is this way. She senses when a kicker is the only solution to the prevailing, unappreciative attitude. A feeling in her bones, she says. A want from within herself. A steadily escalating desire. For the kicker enjoys the same anticipation others have for the Second Coming. Kicker fans study weather charts, they follow the antics of the jet stream, hope for the specialized violence between moody low pressure cells and the bulwark of arctic air. It is here my Minniesorta friend detaches from the Modern Age. She builds little altars, she does not know why. Ice cubes stacked in pyramidal shapes. She drips cat blood or skewers mice with darning needles and lifts their beating little hearts to pound frantically against the cold ice and in its last warm mortality enter the cube where it lays frozen. And then the red-haired Minniesorta ices a tall glass of home-canned tomato juice, with salt, diced celery, pepper and dill pickle; she drinks the thing down at her leisure. It is time for a kicker and she has done her best to bring it. Time for a lesson in pagan snow.

When the kicker comes, my friend laughs, a nervous laugh, laughs as the world falls to its knees before the white-maned kicker. Blizzard warnings rollick her heart. She burps and smells of mouse vitals. She laughs as the storm closes airports, laughs at snarled traffic, laughs as the sky empties of airplanes, the highways stand vacant, schools close, laughs as she kindles a fire in a musty stone chimney. She cackles, my red-haired friend, at radio reports and all the meetings cancelled. She giggles as she fills the bird feeder and pulls the drapes closed and lights her one kerosene lamp somewhere in the bowels of Minniesorta. The world gone quiet and still, as a snowdrift muffles the twentieth century. A day bitten right out of modernism. She blesses the night, the storm, the thorough dark of it. Once, out of glee, she threw off her clothes and ran naked around the house. No one saw. It was safe to do and she knew why and thanked the kicker again.

If you enjoyed

*B*ook *of* Plough

Call our toll-free number
800/366-3091
or write to

Lost River Press, Inc.
P.O. Box 620
Boulder Junction, WI 54512

to find out more about our other titles concerning nature and the
outdoor experience.

We welcome your questions and comments about our products, and urge you to let
us know how we might better serve you.